POWER AND BEAUTY
IMAGES OF
WOMEN IN ART

GEORGES DUBY
MICHELLE PERROT

POWER AND BEAUTY
IMAGES OF
WOMEN IN ART

TAURIS PARKE BOOKS, LONDON

Jacket (front) :
The Red Fish *(detail)*,
Gustav Klimt, 1901-02,
Solothurn, Art Museum

Jacket (back) :
Young Maid (detail),
fresco, late 2nd Century BC,
Pompeii, Villa of Mysteries

This edition first published by
Tauris Parke Books
45 Bloomsbury Square, London WC1A 2HY
in association with KEA Publishing Services Ltd., London

First published as *Images de Femmes* © Plon, Paris 1992

Translation © KEA Publishing Services Ltd. 1992

The Cataloguing in Publication Data for this book is available
from the British Library, London

ISBN 1-85043-612-6

Translated from the French by Berlitz Translation Services
Copyedited by Betty Palmer
Typeset by DQP, 62 Cowcross Street, London EC1M 6BP
Printed in France

CONTENTS

SOCIETY DEPICTED

THE MIDDLE AGES 69
CHIARA FRUGONI

FROM THE SKY TO THE EARTH

6TH-18TH CENTURIES 103
JOËL CORNETTE

CREATORS, CREATED

19TH-20TH CENTURIES   139
ANNE HIGONNET

Images of Women

Georges Duby

Historians work above all with texts. They collect words and phrases, they read. They listen to the voices of earlier times as set down in contemporary writings. However, in the last twenty-five years history has vastly broadened its scope; it is no longer primarily concerned with events but with the undercurrents which sustain and explain them. Influenced by two disciplines which have developed rapidly alongside it – semiotics, which helps us to interpret visual signs, and archaeology, whose dazzling progress has brought to light many artefacts from past generations – the historian has become more and more an observer of objects and images which often teaches us as much as, if not more than, the written word. This book, which originated as the sixth and last volume of a scholarly *Histoire des femmes*, presents a selection from what remains accidentally preserved of those collections of images which our society, western society, sees as history's portrayal of femininity at any given moment. Using a few examples we propose to show how systems of images, meticulously reconstructed, enable us to complement or sometimes to correct what parallel texts teach us.

However, it soon becomes apparent that this complementary material, these different types of portrayal, drawings, sculptures, frescos, paintings, graffiti, photographs, prints, need to be checked very carefully. The historian must verify this material in much the same way as written sources, using whatever methods may be appropriate.

First of all we must ascertain the conditions under which images were created at any given period, remembering that the development of visual conventions followed its own largely autonomous path alongside social changes. On the other hand, this formal development is very much linked to the history of the artistic professions, dependent in their turn on studio traditions held in place by accepted practices which were sometimes modified and sometimes abruptly overthrown by revolutionary innovations.

It is important to remember that the artisans who were attempting to portray femininity worked with live models less frequently than one might think. Usually they worked from copies handed down from generation to generation. It was only when the public demanded something new that they had to renew the standardized patterns from time to time, but they did so carefully, little by little. Certainly culture shock sometimes forced them to accept exotic forms, for example in Gaul under the Romans, when naked Venuses and Dianas embellished wealthy houses in the cities and rural villas. Sometimes the cultural graft took, more often it did not. The historian attempting to get to the truth must carefully measure the dose of realism which each period expected of its image-makers. The demand varied, for reasons which are not clear. Most of the time the dose was weak.

Take the Middle Ages. For centuries societies eschewed human figuration, allowing only abstractions of animals and plants: they produced almost no images of women. Then for centuries after, she appears in symbolic terms only, stereotypical emblems of a certain idea of women. Therefore we must resign ourselves to the fact that we will never know what was the real face, the real body of Heloïse or Eleanor of Aquitaine. Then, during the course of the 14th century, what the artist's eye saw crept more and more into the heart of the formal system of which he was still a prisoner and began to free him from it. He became used to identifying individual characteristics and to reproducing them: the first portraits began to appear. Nevertheless, those svelte girls, like elegant pure-bred greyhounds, with which the Limburg brothers peopled the orchards of the *Très Riches Heures* were undoubtedly inspired by the mannerist inflections of late Gothic art, as well as by the lop-sidedness, which the material itself had, shortly before, imposed on ivory carvings of the Virgin and Child. And if in the sculptures of Arnolfo di Cambio you see heavy, majestic, matronly figures, it is because Arnolfo drew his inspiration from recently discovered Etruscan effigies. It cannot be assumed that Florentine or Parisian women of the 1400s necessarily possessed similar silhouettes.

We must also ask ourselves, when looking at each image, what function it was intended to fulfil by those who decided on its composition. Works of art of the 20th century are surely the first to fulfil no function at all, presenting themselves as pure objects of aesthetic delight. All those which preceded them had a particular intention, meant something, were there for a purpose. In private they served the purpose of enabling two separate beings to communicate, maintaining the memory of a dead person or an absent lover; or perhaps the saints which princes at the end of the Middle Ages commissioned to be painted on folding altar screens (and which reproduction processes, becoming gradually less expensive, soon brought into the most humble of homes) would encourage the spirit of devotion; or as in the case of the image of the Lady with the Unicorn or that of Marilyn Monroe, they might compensate for frustrations, rekindle ardour, colour dreams. When the image was public it was and still is used to help spread a doctrine, proclaim an ideal, publicize a regulation or simply to promote some product or other. The creators were therefore encouraged in their choice of form, attitude and decoration to reinforce the symbol's persuasive power. It was necessary for François Rude, for example, to accentuate the strength of a certain image of a woman in his celebrated relief for the Arc de Triomphe, *La Marseillaise*; in other contexts artists will be found emphasizing the gracious fragility, tenderness, feminine attributes which men in general are seduced by. In any case, depending on the role it had been given – and

Venus squatting, Greek art, 5th Century. Rhodes

Images of Women

—
11

that is why the historian must not fail to question this role beforehand –
the image altered reality, remodelled it, moulded it in one direction or
another, in short more or less deformed it.

It is also important to remember that these images which usually
appear to us in isolation were in fact part of a coherent group of signs
which the historian must attempt to reconstruct before using one
particular fragment to attempt to decipher the reality of relationships
within society. Close links united these paintings, sculptures, engravings,
photographs to one another and linked them again to other kinds of
images. Different visual images were offered by the various forms of
entertainment: ballet, parades, tableaux vivants, fashion shows, theatre.
Mental images, also, were spread by books, the press, sermons. Is it
possible to explain the difference between the women painted by
Boucher and those David painted without bringing into play the
concurrent evolution of opera buffa?

As far as women are concerned, any proper criticism of the
sources in question must take into account one important crucial fact.
Until very recently images, like texts and without doubt even more so,
were with rare exceptions produced by men. Women did not portray
themselves, they were portrayed. Of course, a handful of women did slip
into the circle of painters, sculptors and decorators in all periods. But
generally speaking, as far as the creation of images is concerned, women
have been confined to a marginal role. Throughout all the stages of its
history, our society and probably all societies in the world encouraged
them to enhance the home by working at decorating it. The appearance
of the domestic surroundings and of the body were always essentially a

Les Très Riches Heures of
the Duc du Berry,
Purgatory, *miniature
by the brothers of
Limbourg, circa 1410.
Chantilly, Condé Museum*

woman's domain. Girls were brought up to play this role: in their education, needlework, embroidery, lacemaking, everything traditionally classed as women's work always played an important role. Feminine hands did frequently co-operate in making images which we study today, but usually they carried out the task, rather than conceiving the design. If it is almost certain that English women of Kent embroidered the Bayeux Tapestry, it is equally certain that the arrangements of the successive scenes of this amazing comic strip were devised by men and that in the sewing room, throughout their work, the women submitted docilely to men's orders.

It is possible to cite works carried out entirely by women, such as the strange illuminations to the text of the visions of Hildegard of Bingen which German nuns composed and painted. But make no mistake, they are rarities. Up until very recent times the bourgeoisie were happy to see women fill their idle hours by dabbling in watercolours, just as they played the piano, to entertain and be a credit to their fathers or husbands. But if one of them decided to go further, and she managed to cross the forbidden territory and reach the realm of creative genius, she was singled out, denounced as eccentric, rejected in the same way as those who showed their lesbianism too openly. As a result, in the entire history of painting, sculpture and architecture in the West, only a few women emerge and they are always relegated to a secondary position. One would have to be blinded by prejudice to place Berthe Morisot on a level with Manet, to discover powerful originality in the sculptures of Camille Claudel. Female figures fill the work of Hogarth, Daumier, Gavarni, Forain. How many women before Claire Bretécher caricatured men? Or women? And things do not appear to have changed much these days. In

Young women at the piano, *Silvestro Lega, 1867. Florence, Gallery of Modern Art*

— Rien au monde, vois-tu, n'est charmant comme la femme !...
— D'un autre.

'Here and there',
Paul Gavarni, circa 1840.
Paris, Carnavalet Museum
('Nothing in the world,
don't you see, is as
delightful as woman!'
'Another's!')

Agrippine,
Claire Bretécher, 1987
('Mozart – it's nothing but
film music')

Images of Women

contrast to fiction writing, early overrun by women, and apart from certain areas such as film or photography, the creation of images is one of the areas of our culture in which male domination is the most complete. Even today, it is the male eye which looks at women. The portrayals which enable us to deepen our knowledge of the history of women provide us with very few which are not men's vision of femininity.

That said, there is more than enough material. Since the dawn of history, women have been the preferred subject of the image-makers, and the researcher has a mass of evidence which can be exploited in two ways. It can give us a glimpse of women in the past in their everyday material life, or it can be used to attempt to discern the mental image of women which has evolved in the imagination over the ages. In the first instance the documents of this type are fairly instructive depending on the amount of realism which they contain. When this is an important element, it is direct, raw evidence, almost as reliable as the remains excavated by archaeologists. Like the jewels, the combs, the keys, the needles, which are discovered in burial places or at the sites of deserted villages, they show how women were dressed, how they looked after their homes, what equipment they had, and this enables us to guess their actual actions.

It also reveals a little about women's social position in relation to men. But here the distance is greater when one looks at the reality in which they lived. What the raw image suggests, for example, the juxtaposition of the husband and the wife on an ancient funeral stele, the way in which the male and female donors are arranged at a votive table, or the family members in a marriage photograph, is, as in the order of a

Images of Women

procession or formal rules of precedence, conspicuous and conforming to the good order which society intends to preserve or institute. Ideological presuppositions and consequently the weight of power, this public power which was entirely in the hands of men, have already strongly intervened. We must take more note of this power, if we do not want to be misled when we look at images, because the image is exclusively masculine. Nothing comes from the other side, the other camp, no information allowing us to reconstruct a sort of self-portrait of the women of former times, the vision which they had of themselves, and which, as a counterbalance, would be useful in allowing an equilibrium to be established. Therefore we must content ourselves with what men modelled; and indeed, this is of great interest in order to have an understanding of the relationship between the masculine and the feminine. Because these countless images, this extremely rich fund of documents, bring to light the three obsessional images which have haunted the male spirit whenever he thought of women: the image of the female partner in the games of love, that of mother protector and consoler (and it is here that the immense, formidable power of women comes to light), then finally as a defensive reaction, that of the mate, indispensable although rigorously kept in a subordinate and submissive position.

Study for Venus Anadyomene, *Jean-Dominique Ingres, c. 1840. Montauban, Ingres Museum.*

The first of these figures occupies the largest part of the field. It can even be said that it totally invades it, as it is constantly visible just beneath the surface in the two others. In fact for all the men who have painted, sculpted, engraved or simply drawn or sketched, and for all those who wanted to view the image of woman, her body, object of lust and subject of dread, was apparently the subject *par excellence*. Whether oversimplified, reduced to the intertwining of a few lines on the most humble of amulets, as in graffiti where obsessions are spontaneously displayed, or lovingly detailed, using the most refined techniques of great art in order to celebrate the delights of feminine forms, the thread continues right throughout history. However, over the ages these forms have been imagined, and therefore seen, by the image makers in constantly changing aspects, each period creating its own rules, its own laws, its ideal of bodily perfection. These variations were determined by a number of factors, which we need to be more familiar with. Whatever the reasons, it would appear that the dominant impulse came from male interests. It was men who modelled women's bodies and also the wardrobe designed to cover and adorn them: clothes, hairstyles, cosmetics and jewellery were in fact inseparable from the flesh which they concealed and revealed at the same time, and their purpose was to increase attractiveness according to the tastes of the period. The history of the images of women is therefore closely linked to the history of fashion, which largely falls outside our scope;

Images of women

but it was not, as now, governed by the despots of haute couture and the market demands of the rag trade. These models were always designed within the orbits of powerful men, and styled to increase their prestige. To this end princes and patricians exhibited their women, decked in their most brilliant finery, surrounding them like the other items in their treasury. And we can be sure that replicas of these exemplary lines generally spread very quickly from top to bottom of the fabric of society.

However, the portrayals suggested in painting, sculpture, engraving, also depended no less directly on the general aesthetics of the period: there is an obvious relation between the style of various imaginary artistic forms and the female shape. The look is also linked to public morality and the role it currently assigned to wives and daughters. There have been times and places where the preference was to portray women as intrepid Amazons, as fighters, others where the image of the mother of the family prevailed, still others where the main reference was to the passive odalisque in the darkness of forbidden chambers, and, under pressure of the predominant code of behaviour, the desired body took on a given appearance in the hands of the image maker. Finally the temperament of the artist and the person the work was being carried out for also played a role. The contrast between the ample generosity of the late Renoirs and the febrile neuroticism of Kirchner's nudes was not only due to the very different cultures of Paris and Berlin at the turn of the century. And who can say whether the perverse emphasis which Cranach the Elder gave to the slender contours of adolescent bodies was imposed by his own fantasies or by those of the Elector of Saxony whose longings he was satisfying?

Salomé dancing before Herod,
Gustave Moreau, 1876.
Paris, Gustave Moreau
Museum

So it is important for the historian to establish whether a particular portrayal of a female body was painted, sculpted, engraved in order to be shown publicly, to all and sundry, or on the contrary to be locked away in a place with controlled access; or even if it was circulated clandestinely, ending up shut away as *The Origins of the World* by Courbet was, concealed by the green curtain which Khalil Bey, who owned the work, opened from time to time in front of the most intimate visitors to his study. In fact, women's bodies have not been shown equally freely over time and in the various regions of western culture. At this point conventions regarding modesty and of the forbidden entered into play and protected her. Accustomed as we are to the broadest licence, it is easy to forget the power of the forbidden and the weight it carried until very recently. When André Masson disembarked in the USA in 1942, New York customs officials thought that the drawings in his luggage were an affront to public morals and confiscated them, and less than 20 years ago in Paris, it was apparently considered indecent to exhibit openly certain engravings by Picasso – they were kept apart, confined to an annexe of the gallery, a sort of 'hell' reserved for the initiated.

From this point of view, the evolution of the nude in the plastic arts is revealing. It illustrates the place allocated to women's bodies in the value system, which means to women themselves (but one must tread most carefully here in the maze of particularly entangled relationships). The nude – and in our civilization we are talking almost exclusively of the female nude – had spread everywhere under the Roman Empire. When the culture of antiquity foundered it was repressed, as a result of a strong tendency in certain leading circles to reject any portrayal of the human form. The urge was especially fierce among the evangelizers determined to destroy the statues of false gods, to tear down everything which could sustain the memory of paganism. This took place within the spread of a Christianity entirely dominated by monks, men for whom virginity was of supreme worth, fornication the worst of sins, who considered women to be the incarnation of absolute evil and strove only to see in her body a repugnant bag of excrement. The eclipse lasted for centuries, apparently with general concurrence, and during this time decent women only left the home swathed in cloth, veiled, hair chastely covered. It was only in literature that deep aesthetic characteristics, escaping the church's control, were revealed. Both the obscenities in humorous stories and the discreet silences of courtly lyrics illustrated the reserve which chivalrous society showed to feminine nudity. The love songs, the romances, were loath to divest the beloved lady or the sorceress of the robes and petticoats which hid her charms. The hero imagines them, he burns to unveil them, but if he gets to the stage of doing it, he is modestly silent. And the statues of their loves which, according to the storytellers, Tristan and Hector had placed in the 'chamber of beauties' where they withdrew for amorous devotions, were not undressed.

As for sacred art, Holy Writ sometimes forced it to show the naked bodies of women, when illustrating the story of Genesis or the description of the Last Judgement. But then it applied itself to neutralizing them, reducing them to abstract symbols, stripping them of all seductiveness, even attempting to debase them, to make them contemptible, evocative of bestiality and inescapable corruption. A change could be detected in the middle of the 13th century, when on one of the tympana of Bourges Cathedral, female bodies free from the marks of sin appeared for the first time; they were those of the Risen, gaily bursting forth from the tomb, supple, delicate, reconciled. Fifty years later, using the same theme, Giotto installed on the walls of the Arena Chapel at Padua the first sensuous nudes in European painting. From then on it was like a vibrant dawn, while high culture, disengaging itself little by little from the hold of the Church, discovered that nature was not so bad after all, that it was acceptable to enjoy life's pleasures without feeling guilty, enjoyed a whirl of celebrations, and began to admire the rediscovered relics of ancient sculptures. From then on any pretext was acceptable to glorify the attractiveness of the female body, whether that of the martyred saints, their tender flesh lacerated by their executioners, or of penitent sinners whose bodies were also bruised. The body of Eve, obviously, was among them. Van Eyck observed it intimately in all its carnal truth; Ghiberti glorified it, nascent, spring-like, triumphant. And with the Renaissance in full swing, pretexts were no longer necessary; once again artists dared to portray the bodies of goddesses, initially copying Roman statues until the painter risked placing his easel in front of the naked body of a model.

From the 16th century, the nude became an artistic genre in the same way as a still life or a landscape, but was given much more prestige; it freely provided the artist with the material from which to develop his ideas and it was a delectable subject to the art lover. The subject invaded high art, the great history paintings, in Venice, in Florence, in Rome and in Antwerp. Spain obstinately resisted the nude, only allowing the female

Eve, *Lucas Cranach, 14th Century, Florence, Uffizi*

body if concealed; less reticent, the Dutch attempted to moralize it. It was in fact treated in many different ways according to the spirit of the place, the nature of the commission and the constraints of an art trade which was continually spreading. Thus the range declined throughout modern times; the serene simplicity, the radiance, the candidness of the composition of a Blanchard or a Vouet, even compared to the libertine freedom, the shamelessness of the crumpled underclothes of a Greuze, can add nothing to the shuddering ecstasy which Abraham Bloemaert imprinted 50 years earlier on the dejected body of Mary Magdalene.

Germany remained naïve and prudish to the end of the 19th century. In France, however, under the Second Empire and the Third Republic, while the men of the ruling classes made strict demands on ladies' and girls' modesty and reticence (but still allowed themselves to keep dancers and frequent brothels), official art was more frank. With the blessing of the Institute, nudity appeared everywhere – on the sides of monuments, on the cornices of salons and even on the ceiling of the Salle Liard in the Sorbonne, a place strictly devoted to erudite learning – blatant cascades of breasts and rumps displayed as if to expose the sham of bourgeois prudishness. Great painters, like Manet, Lautrec, Picasso, Bonnard, exploited this freedom in their own way. In fact they did so in moderation, looking clearly at woman's naked body, observing her indirectly like a dangerous enemy, watching carefully to defend themselves against her magic spell, her imperfections, her weaknesses, and taking pleasure in emphasizing what her appearance revealed about aggressive power. Sometimes, completely detached, they treated her simply as a beautiful object, exposed, like a bouquet of sunflowers or the

iridescent surface of a pond, to subtle plays of light and changes in colour. Nowadays, the nude in art hardly exists any more, partly because for a long time painting and sculpture have had nothing new to say, but particularly because at the end of the second millennium it has become natural in the West to be naked, both for women and for men.

At the heart of masculine consciousness, woman is also, is perhaps even primarily, mother. The longed-for mother, the rejected mother, fountain of life, ultimate recourse, refuge. The vigour of this imaginary model explains the presence, so frequent in the memory of families, at the mythical root of their lineage, of a founding female ancestor who merges into the earth at the point where the dynasty takes root. It explains why patriarchal societies willingly yield to matriarchs, when they have been freed by widowhood, when age has stripped from them whatever terror femininity holds, a certain power, in particular the one that they wield over their son, established at his side as valued advisers, assisting him to manage the patrimony. And the vigour of this model also explains why feminine figures occupy such a prominent place among the invisible powers from which one expects healing, prosperity or mediation. This omnipresent, omnipotent phantasm thus establishes itself at the source of so many images of women, majestic, imposing, resolute, seated, in the peaceful exercise of their moral magistracy, on this high place which recalls to mind the fecundity which they have shown in their time. Images of ancestors showing their descendants an example of domestic virtue, images of regents presented for the people to respect, and lastly guardian images of mother goddesses. The latter loom up from the depths of ages past and their lineage extends as far as the effigies of the guardian saints

L'Ile de France, *Aristide Maillol, 1910. Paris, Museum of the Petit Palais*

Images of women

adopted by cities at the height of the Middle Ages, extends as far as these idols, covered with gold and cameos, ensconced in grottoes in the glow of candles to overawe the pilgrims of the year 1000.

So necessary were they, and gifted with such a robust ascendancy, that they succeeded in replacing the statues of pagan divinities which Christianity had hoped to destroy. Christianity, monotheistic and moreover, during these times, fundamentally misogynist, had in effect succeeded, though not without difficulty, in casting out the goddesses whom earlier religions of Europe had coupled with male gods. Under pressure from popular devotions, however, Christianity had to tolerate the cult of a Saint Genevieve, of a Saint Foy. But if the system of beliefs, at the heart of which our culture has been formed, attaches such importance to femininity in the final count, it is because it organizes itself around the figure of a god made man, whom a woman carried in her womb and brought into this world without losing her virginity, and who by his incarnation has become the brother of us all. Christian piety therefore naturally gravitated towards the mother of God, placing her on a level scarcely below that of Christ the Son, as illustrated in the Coronation scene which became established on the portals of French cathedrals at the end of the 12th century. For generations for the whole of Christianity and, after the Reformation, for a large part of it still, the image of Mary was a sublime one of untarnished femininity, made all the more fascinating by the fact that, as a consequence of the metaphor likening the Virgin Mary to the Church, the Bride of Christ, it associated with the values of motherhood and virginity those of sovereign marriage, of a lady empowered to intercede, obedient but tenacious, and finally close to male omnipotence, sweeping it away in order to moderate its rigours. Hence the figure of Our Lady reigns all over European iconography. Above all she is a mother figure, the Virgin and Child making her own body into the throne of God, the Virgin and the Mantle sheltering humanity, frightened children under her wing, the Virgin of Suffering, Mater Dolorosa, prostrate on the body of the condemned man.

In many other images, less intimately linked to religion, women still appear as the begetter. In fact, in these images the characteristics of the female lover emerge more clearly as being those of the mother, for they served the purpose of inflaming men's hearts, of pushing them into action, into surpassing themselves. Hence these feminine images of mother earth, of the motherland. Venice was a woman for the members of the Grand Council, for whom Veronese worked, and for those who commissioned Rude it was vital that French citizens, old and young alike, be moved to take up arms by a beautiful woman. France is a woman on all the monuments to those killed in the Great War, and also in all the Town Halls. So too are the earthly values, charity, strength, temperance, justice and those noble ideas for which men should be prepared to sacrifice themselves. We feel ready to spill our blood for them, just as we would for our mother or lover. Desire, married to nostalgia for the maternal womb. Like Delacroix in 1830, the cameramen who filmed the student demonstrations across the western world in 1968 did not fail to place the figure of a woman, energetic and noble, in the front line of the good struggle.

The Woman and the Puppet,
Félicien Rops, 1877.
Private collection

In daily life, and with the firm intention of preserving the hierarchies that they deemed necessary for the maintenance of social order, men have always persuaded themselves that, if they cannot do without women, then women must be subservient. It is their duty to guide women, if necessary to correct them, to keep a tight rein on them to prevent them from being harmful, so that nothing may erode the natural superiority of the masculine sex. This is what a good number of symbolic portrayals have proclaimed – all those in cemeteries, on votive offerings, on emblems of political power, on wedding portraits, which show the head of the family and his wife together. It was important that she appear close to him in public, as she would be in her own place in private, in the conjugal bed. She must appear on his right as a cherished assistant, ornate, on show, to demonstrate how her man's power is based on the institution of marriage. Often the image-makers were required to emphasize the equality which must lie at the heart of the matrimonial association, so they presented husband and wife seated side by side, like Christ and Mary in the Coronation scene. But even when he is not assured of his power, his whole figure towering over her, we sense from the gentleness in her look, the languor which presses down on her and makes her huddle up to her appointed protector, that it is her fate to be dominated.

The Dream, *Pablo Picasso, 1932. New York, Victor W. Ganz Collection*

Indeed, this is what men want, whether consciously or not: to establish that woman is by nature weak. In reality they are afraid of her. This unpredictable stranger worries them. Therefore they want her to be less robust than they are, flexible, subjected to the constraints they place on her. They have reinforced this conviction through images, hoping to convince woman herself that her fragility is her strength, that all her

Images of women

—

30

charms stem from this and from her powerful weapon seduction, which subdues the other sex. Is not beauty, her main preoccupation, primarily sensitivity, grace, delicacy? And it is because she is supple, tender, because she is gentle, not rough, stiff, brittle, that she maintains that hold over the male which her weakness forces her to cede to him. The images have returned to this idea incessantly, pointedly, anchoring women to that major function which men intended to make them responsible for: to introduce around men, as a counterbalance to their coarseness, their seriousness, to the violence which they claimed to monopolize, lightness, gentleness, frivolity, imagination. And if men conceded that women have a serious side, or some small measure of initiative, it is only in relation to domestic duties. Managing the interior of the home is left to her. That is woman's domain. It is proper that she remains confined to this.

To a large extent, iconography served the purpose of restricting woman to these roles. I am thinking here of the painters popular in 18th-century France. Watteau's woman plays on elegance, Boucher's on sensuality; for Fragonard, it is that spiritedness whose piquancy was appreciated by men during salon conversations. But look at the women painted by Chardin: they manage the household, supervise the children's education, they attend to everything discreetly and diligently. Because they are considered fragile, women have the right to be cared for. Above all they ask for protection. They are counted among those precious possessions which must be held tightly to protect them from harm. They cannot defend themselves. It is up to men to defend them, to take on the attackers who encircle this prey, ready to seize it. How many propaganda posters have shown women as the intended victims, as small children are

shown too. Threatened, unarmed, pushed into the nursery. Down the ages, images have perpetuated the notion of a fundamental incapacity in women, surrendering, passive, dressed up for men's pleasure. Are we then to believe that images have ceased to do so today when, undoubtedly, the liberated woman appears to men to be more formidable than ever? A clear-sighted analysis of images in the mass media, of those which invade our television screens or are placed primarily for women to look at in magazines targeted at women, would be ready evidence of the permanence of an unshakeable machismo whose insidious persuasiveness is still singularly effective. Indeed, the vision of women offered to them in these images, cloaked in what remains of courtesy and gallantry in our world, actually flatters rather than displeases them.

La Pensée,
Auguste Rodin, 1886.
Paris, Rodin Museum

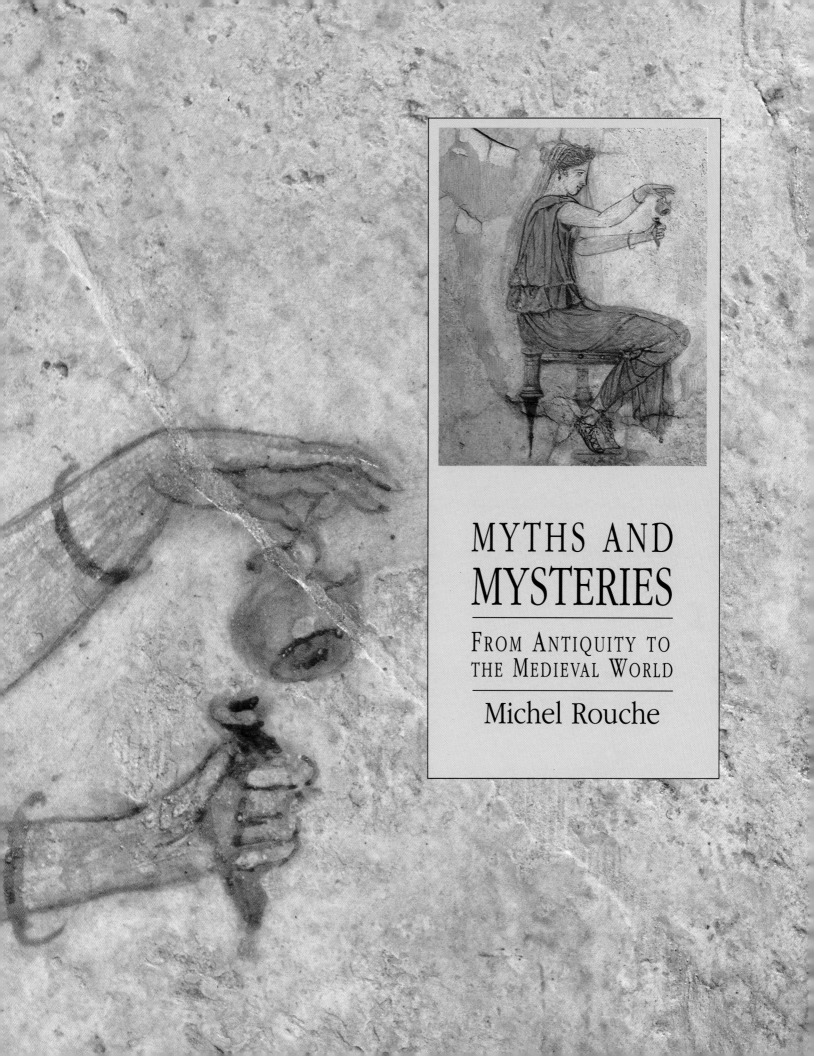

MYTHS AND MYSTERIES

FROM ANTIQUITY TO THE MEDIEVAL WORLD

Michel Rouche

From antiquity to the Middle Ages, woman passes from myth to mystery. Inexplicably, she invigorates narrative or images, bearing the message of knowledge. The myths of the ancients brought knowledge to bear on the big questions concerning the beginning and the end. Their replies put the female sex at the forefront. Each myth reveals and isolates one of the feminine functions, separating it from the others. Life and death are two women, one the mother goddess bearing and recreating the child, the future of humanity; the other the priestess of war, assuring survival through human sacrifice. Each of them, whether mistress of life's origins or its end, now benefactor, now bringer of evil, is at the hands of destiny. It is the myth of the preserver-destroyer, who is obliged to kill so that others may live. Other feminine figures are all powerful, some over the future, some over knowledge, others in turn over sex. These last figures above all, frivolous, fickle, fantastic, inspire in men a crazy, raging, wild love. The mistress is worse than a mantis.

Among all these myths Rome gave a privileged place to the ideal of the matron given over to her reproductive role in order to construct society, and expelled to its fringes the Dionysian lover, obsessed with her body and socially disruptive in her lust for men. The pagan mythology of women hence presents images of a collective subconscious which rejects history, denies liberty, and displays anguish before this spouse who cannot be assimilated, majestic matron or greedy Gorgon. These portrayals attempt to reduce women to their lowest common denominators: procreation, conversation, pleasure. Mother, wife, or whore, each has its own exclusive role. Death versus love, child versus lover, these contradictory urges of pagan wisdom reduce woman to her component fragments.

With the Christian mysteries a subtle shift in feminine power takes place. Woman is called upon to rediscover a unity lost in the opposition between her constructive and her destructive roles. The mystery is a blinding light which obliterates the myth and reassembles the feminine functions which had been scattered. New associations appear in images: wife and mother, virgin and mother, wife and virgin. The first shows a new couple with union becoming more important than procreation. The

Preceding pages

*Woman pouring perfume
into a bottle,
fresco from a villa in
Farnesina,
1st Century. Rome,
Museum of the Therms*

Myths and mysteries

second, madonna or martyr, offers the choice to say yes or no, marking the giddying prospect of liberty taking the place of destiny. The last offers trapped queens, amorous nuns, barren wives, under their veils of linen or of their own hair, the opportunity to make sexual ecstasy part of their spiritual or carnal unions.

Through these classic images, this step towards reintegration allows for the end of the obsession with procreation (the biblical Susanna and Theutberga, rejected for her childlessness), the glorification of the woman who says yes (Mary) or no (Saint Agnés), the demand for political human sacrifices (Eleanor of Aquitaine), and the recovery of lost innocence (Mary Magdalene). When the virgin can be decked with imperial finery, the whore can be unveiled and the mother put to the test, their power becomes an authority of a new prophetic kind. Beyond their saintliness, they issue a command. These medieval women turned towards the other, or the Other, are the first to swing humanity away from destruction towards construction by repeating 'unite'.

Goddess-mother, stone statuette, 1st Century. Alice-Sainte-Reine, Alesia Museum

Myths and mysteries

From left to right

Venus of Laussel, also called Woman with Bison's horn, Aurignacian period, 20,000 BC. Bordeaux, Musée d'Aquitaine

Venus of Grimaldi, Neolithic period. Saint-Germain-en-Laye, Museum of National Antiquities

Venus, called Venus of Willendorf, Aurignacian Period, 33000-8000 BC. Vienna, Museum of Natural History

Mother goddesses, war priestesses

Who says sex says sections, says man and woman, says death and life. While Neanderthal man (80,000-30,000 BC) thought he had resolved the problem of his own end by inventing funeral rituals, modern man looked into his origins. Where did he come from? From woman! The evidence was such that the hunters of the Upper Palaeolithic age sculpted the bringer of life before any other form of artistic manifestation. Those idols which appeared first of all in the Orient, then in Europe and particularly in Aquitaine in the Périgord (30,000-16,000 BC), proclaimed the astonished ecstasy of the stone-carver before the strangeness of the different being who unfolds in his hands, before his eyes. These statues, whether of spindly form or grossly swollen, all have deliberately exaggerated sexual characteristics. Through the life which is developing, the buttocks and stomach grow larger, the breasts grow rounder, the nipples crack. The head remains strangely hollow, transformed into a third breast or even covered with little curls. These hint at other hairs, pubic hairs, suggested by dots. The material, finely grained limestone, green steatite, brown amber, suggests the taught skin of the belly, at once smooth and bumpy. The horn of plenty, which the Lady of Laussel is holding, is also the crescent of the moon which reigns over her. But on this occasion she is brandishing it triumphantly to show that she dominates this cosmos which ceaselessly drifts by. These idols are small enough to be held in the hand, gentle to the touch, shiny and polished. For the Palaeolithic primitive already knows that the skin of the pregnant woman is worth all the marble of the idols to come.

For the woman of proto-historic times, passing from giver of life to priestess of death represents almost the same steps. When it was discovered at Vix, near to the Roman Gaulish town of Mont Lassois, this bronze urn had impressive dimensions, 1.50m wide, 1.64m high, weight 208kg, and capacity 1200l. It was near a dismantled chariot on to which it could be loaded. It was also near the body of a young woman of thirty to thirty five, decorated with sumptuous jewels. The Greek or Etruscan urn dates back to 500-480 BC. For what diplomatic purpose would foreigners have offered this gigantic 'wine bribe' to a princess? The truth is something quite different as the geographer Strabo reveals, when he describes the rites of a Germanic people very close to the Gauls (*Germani* means 'brothers of the Celts'): 'Their women who went to war with them, were accompanied by sacred female soothsayers. The soothsayers had white hair, were dressed in white, fastened gauze scarves round their shoulders, wore bronze belts, walked barefoot. Armed with a dagger, they went through the camp to meet the prisoners. They crowned them and led them towards a bronze urn with a large capacity. They had a rostrum on which each of them climbed so that they could stand over the cauldron and slit the throat of each prisoner who had been hoisted up. From the flow of blood which gushed into the urn, they made a prediction.'[1] The priestess buried with her urn is represented here on the lid. Unmoving and hieratic she dominates the scene unfolding at her feet with an ironic Mona Lisa smile. But her right wrist and the thumb and fingers of her left hand have been deliberately broken. Why?

Bronze urn of Vix and
its lid topped with a kora,
6th Century BC.
Châtillon-sur-Seine,
Archaeological Museum
of Châtillon

The answer is provided by the Celtic cauldron of Gundestrup (100-50 BC), and the Gorgon-head handles of the urn of Vix itself. The Gaulish torque (necklace) with a ball at each end which the priestess is wearing can be found again round the neck of the goddess, while her Greek-Etruscan homologue is sticking out her tongue to predict death, and held closely by two serpents hissing around her head. In fact it is the priestess of death whose carnivorous mask with its clutching arms drains the victims of their prophetic blood. Only a virgin, pure because of her blond-white hair, her white veil, could read the destiny of her tribe in the dregs of blood in this gigantic vat, then make each warrior drink from the cup which she filled from her pouring vase with a mixture of the red juice of the vine and the liqueur of life. Thus she produced a holy frenzy, unleashed the ecstatic savagery which would give the predicted victory. In contrast to the Palaeolithic Venuses, whose heads are silent while their wombs prepare to bring forth their living loads, the prophetess

Myths and mysteries

of Vix with her empty virginal womb spits out death from her lips, her tongue, her eyes and her teeth. She has power over the gods below. Only she can arouse the death-wish in man. One can understand that this female destroyer conjured up shudders of horror. Once she was interned in her burial mound, would not her spirit become incarnate in her statuette on the top of the urn and come back for more sacrifice? That can be averted. Someone broke her hands to prevent them from cutting any more throats.

Gorgon (left), urn of Vix, 6th Century BC. Châtillon-sur-Seine, Archeological Museum of Châtillon

Celtic goddess wearing a torque (right), vestiges in gilded silver of the cauldron of Gundestrup. Copenhagen, National Museum

Myths and mysteries

*The Three Majestic
Goddesses (left), relief
carved by Phlegon.
Lyon, Museum of Gallo-
Roman Civilization*

Full or empty, saviour or killer, pagan woman is powerful. These two groups of mother goddesses discovered in Burgundy, one of which is also from the Vix region in the heart of Gaul, date from the 1st and 2nd centuries AD. At first sight the three Augustan mothers (the dedication which their maker Phlegon engraved for them) are identical. The only thing which distinguishes them from one another is the number of apples, one, two or three, and the horn of plenty held by the middle figure. This sort of repetition would only serve to increase the effect. But would showing the same figure three times merely be a tripling of the mother goddesses' ability to give prosperity generously to men? As the second sculpture proves, this is not so at all. The three goddesses have three functions, those possessed by each and every woman in Celtic society and in every Indo-European society in general. This division into three functions concerns men as well as women; priestess, warrior and nurse. At the centre, the first function, that of the druid (meaning 'very scholarly' in Gaulish) is symbolized by the book which she unrolls in her hands. To the right the second function, that of the warrior who is also king, is signified by the circle of sky and the globe that the queen is holding. To the left, the third function is indicated by the posture of the nurse: her crossed legs and closed thighs show that she is not the mother. She is feeding the child that she holds swaddled in her arms. All three are mistresses of destiny; hence their name, Fatae, which gave us fairies. Whether they are called Morgana or Bridget, these goddesses of the battlefield are barely revealing their breasts, because if they were exposed they would seduce and paralyse the men's war-like fury. It is a discreet reminder of their triple power: knowledge, strength, pleasure.

*The three Goddess-Mothers
(right), stone from
Vertault, 1st-2nd
Centuries. Châtillon-sur-
Seine, Archaeological
Museum of Châtillon*

Myths and mysteries

Marriages

In Indo-European civilizations there is no word to denote marriage. The Roman world used the word *matrimonium* to denote the event of the woman becoming mother. But in the same way that patrimonium denoted patrimony, matrimony alluded to the possessions of the bride. A Roman marriage was therefore above all a contract to create a function, an alliance of two hands and of two bodies with a view to making a matron. This is borne out by the signs exchanged by husband and wife on these two funeral sculptures: in the Portogruaro sarcophagus, the couple's right hands are given to one another, while the tablets of the contract symbolize the respective possessions included in property settlement, but which the husband holds in his left hand, for it is he who controls the dowry. In fact, in the eyes of the Romans, the woman is incapable of managing. The iron or gold ring was the symbol of free men. It was put on the left ring-finger because, according to Aulus Gellius, a vein starting from here flowed directly to the heart. The veil which covers the head of the bride is a red-orange colour symbolizing the fire which will burn their senses, purifying them of all passion. Finally, the promise of procreation wells up between the husband and wife, a spirit brandishing the torch of life. This peace treaty (*foedus*) with the two joined hands also representing the promise of no disputes, this faith (a word which comes from *foedus*) signifies strength and fidelity beyond death, since the scene is engraved on a sarcophagus. The woman married out of duty is therefore praised here as a moral matron.

Couple from the Pillar of the Lady with the Ring (left), circa 165. Arlon, Luxembourg Museum.

Marriage scene from a marble sarcophagus (right), 3rd Century. Portogruaro, National Museum

Roman women

Reduced to her role as child-bearer by Roman law, which watched out for any feminine adultery, the matron must ignore desire and banish pleasure. In contrast free women, that is to say those who could not contract a 'just' and legal marriage, emancipated slaves, the rejected, widows and so on, and who aspired to experience something hitherto denied them, could choose a lover and sleep with him (Latin, *concubere*). On this couch, two concubines lie naked under their cover, a dog warming their feet. While the Romans refused to give any legal standing to the practice of concubage, it nevertheless a legal activity. For a woman it was the only means of living according to her own wishes. Whether her liaison was secret or public, she had a lover who served her, took notice of her feelings and her heart. If she was a slave, she might hope to win her emancipation and her freedom, even if it means passing from the bed to the sarcophagus with a beautiful inscription: '[From] Caius the free man, for Gaia whom I freed'. These women who set out to conquer men strengthened Romans in the private conviction that 'a woman's desire is fiercer than a man's'. Their lust is insatiable. They destroy marriages and society. Love is antisocial. Passion is dangerous. The pagan terror of women stems directly from the dichotomy that reserves children to matrons and love to free women. All women are enslaved by one or other of these tasks, even the stoic sirens of friendship, and the two needs cannot be appeased at the same time.

Terracotta bed with a couple, from Bordeaux, 2nd Century. Saint-Germain-en-Laye, Museum of National Antiquities

Christian women

In the 4th century AD, a new portrayal of women slowly appears as Christianity is accepted: here we see a respectable housewife and mother with her two children and a wife with her husband. The inscriptions, both Greek and Latin, read: 'Live piously'. There would seem to be nothing here to distinguish Christian marriage from pagan marriage, but in fact the Greek and oriental source of the motifs on these two gilt glasses points to their being interpreted as Christian. They are part of a series of funeral glasses which evolve imperceptibly from a human and historic portrayal around AD 325 to a symbolic and theological stage at the end of the 4th century. This young widow, her eyes made larger with kohl, wearing a sumptuous costume of the aristocratic classes, is proud of her son and daughter, the girl being even more richly adorned. Here one can guess at the double ideal of the Roman family composed of a reasonable number of children (on other glasses it does not exceed four) and Christian love with the woman 'faithful to one single man'. 'What is astonishing about Christians', said Galen, the pagan doctor to Marcus Aurelius, 'is their sexual restraint, even among the women.' This new image of woman, neither killer nor breeding stock, corresponds to the ideal of marriage, the symbol of the union between Christ and the Church. The injunction to husband and wife to live piously is expressed elsewhere by the figure of Christ crowning man and woman. Pope Leo the Great specified in 451: 'The sacrament of Christ and the Church is the mystery of marriage.' Like the Bride of Christ, the woman walks with her husband, indissolubly and faithfully, towards holiness thanks to carnal union.

Christian family (left), gilt glass of the cross of Desiderio, 4th Century. Brescia, Christian Museum.

Couple (right), gilt glass, paleo-Christian, late 3rd Century. Paris, Museum of the Petit Palais

Frankish women

'Susanna was very beautiful.' Married to Joakim, she was one day interrupted by two old men while bathing in her garden... This rock crystal, engraved by order of King Lothair II of Lorraine (855-69), portrays in nine scenes the drama of the innocent wife held up to slander. She refuses their advances and screams, which brings the servants running. The old men go to the husband, place their hands on the head of Susanna and swear that they have seen her in bed with a man. Condemned to death by stoning, she is brought in for execution when Daniel intervenes. He questions the two old men separately and makes them contradict one another. They are then stoned. This biblical story was at the origin of the cult of Saint Susanna from before 354. The Church promulgated this veneration to prevent the Germanics and Romans from renouncing their wives under the pretext of adultery, a very frequent practice.

Equality in marriage and its indissolubility were illustrated by the punishment of the two accusers and the inviolable closed garden of the wife, not forgetting her self-abnegating silence in the face of her accusers, which is similar to that of Christ before Pilate. Saved by God, Susanna is a victim and an instrument of salvation at one and the same time. The spice of this story is heightened by the fact that Lothair II spent his reign trying to repudiate his wife Theutberga, who was sterile, so that he could marry his concubine who had given him a son. The Church, for which only forced consent and failure to consummate it are grounds for nullifying a marriage, refused. So the king had his wife accused of incest. Pope Nicholas I, the new Daniel, proclaimed Theutberga's innocence. Without an heir, Lorraine was divided. For the first time the honour of a woman was placed above politics.

Myths and mysteries

Virgin martyrs, amorous nuns

Marriage produces virgins. Or so Pope Paschal I (817-824) asserted when he placed this mosaic in the mausoleum of his mother Theodora, portraying her with her head covered in a widow's veil and framed by the square halo reserved for the living. At her side are Saint Praxeda, the Virgin Mary and Saint Pudentia. Even though the two virgin martyrs are mythical, the parallel is an eloquent one. Opposites in paganism, the two states of mother and virgin are complementary here, for they are both the result of a union, one carnal, the other spiritual. Moreover, in order to show that carnal is spiritual, the large mosaic of Saint Agnes, dressed as a Roman Empress, between two popes, Honorius I (625-38) and Symmachus (498-514), suggests what the real power of this woman is. She was the first woman to receive an official cult, from 331, and at the beginning of the 5th century a rich legend proliferated, as a measure of popular veneration. Probably martyred for refusing to renounce her faith, Agnes, condemned according to some to the brothel, according to others to the stake, perished when she was scarcely nubile. Pope Damasus (366-84) specified that before being devoured by the flames, in a reflex action she covered herself in her hair. In a time of pagan mentality, when female nudity was a primitive mating call, Agnes became the symbol of a new sense of decency, founded on respect for the strong woman who says no. With her crown and breastplate of pearls, her body, invisible under the imperial costume, is that of the untouchable woman.

Theodora, (left), Saint Praxeda, the Virgin and Saint Pudentia, 9th-Century mosaic. Rome, Church of Saint Praxeda, Saint Zenon Chapel

Saint Agnes (right), detail from a mosaic, circa 625-638. Rome, Saint Agnes-outside-the-Walls

Myths and mysteries

SCAAGNES

Radegunda, Aldegunda

The new Christian woman is therefore a woman with her own free will. Radegunda, who died in her monastery in Poitiers in 567, like Aldegunda, founder of Maubeuge, who died in 684, were certainly not lacking in autonomy. The former, forced to marry King Clotaire, preferred the mystical 'fires of desire' to 'the gentleness of a mundane marriage'. Wanting with all her might to become a recluse, she is seen imploring Saint Medardus, Bishop of Soissons, to replace the veil. The bishop, taken to one side by the king's officials who reminded him that he could not break a public Christian marriage, ended up with a laying of hands on her. Thus he consecrates her a deaconess, overriding the recent interdiction of the appointed minister in consideration of her strength of character and balanced mysticism. Aldegunda, another amorous nun, refused marriage in order to obtain the mystical Husband, is portrayed here in the form of an angel, dragging her on her knees before Christ's sacrificial altar to show her heaven where her spiritual father, Saint Amandus (who died around 675), has just entered. These visions of Aldegunda, like those of Radegunda, describe a spiritual path in which prayer is expressed like a passionate relationship: the engagement, the temptations of desire for power expressed by Satan, marriage then death, true entry into eternal life, where desire is finally overcome. The vocabulary of carnal love in wedlock is used again nine centuries later by Saint Teresa of Àvila, to describe the passage from carnal gifts to spiritual gifts. 'The Lord has married you so that you receive the incorruptible crown.' If there is a female priesthood or ministry, it is to be found then at the heart of this insatiable craving of the monastic prophetesses whose vow of chastity is no more than a cry of: 'I want You'.

Radegunda (top left), crowned with diadem, visits Saint Medard, Bishop of Noyon. Radegunda (below) is consecrated deaconess by Saint Medard, miniature from the Life of Saint Radegunda, *Fortunat, 10th Century. Poitiers, Municipal Library*

Vision of Saint Aldegunda (right), miniature from Life and Miracle of Saint Amand, *late 11th Century. Valenciennes, Municipal Library*

Virgin saints and holy virgins

Seated on their thrones, the Blessed Virgin Mary and the virgin Saint Foy mark a turning point in the portrayal of victorious women, one defeating sin, the other death. From Carolingian prototypes in wood, these Virgin mothers, black like the much-loved wife of the Song of Songs, and these virgin martyrs in gold, the colour of triumph, spread across the Auvergne, Rouergue, the Toulouse area and Catalonia in the 11th and 12th centuries. The one at Montserrat presents the Child-God, the flesh of his flesh, the Incarnate, 'as in the flesh', a shocking heresy to the Cathars of these regions. The same principle, glorification of the female body (and not idolatry as Bernard d'Angers at one time thought), is found again in the statue of Saint Foy, for it is a reliquary containing the skull of the martyr. This idealized body became an instrument of salvation. Between 984 and 1010 the primitive statue was covered again in gold plate, adorned with antique cameos and studded with jewels. The face, of disproportionate size to the body, is in reality a gold mask of a Roman emperor which was held in front of his face while he climbed victoriously to the Capitol. Now it is the victim of the emperor's persecution who triumphs. At the end of the 16th century, Saint Foy was carried at the head of the Christian army of the King of Aragon, to prove to the Moor, who denied the divinity of Jesus, that a woman died to affirm the faith. These two virgins, neither mother goddess nor warrior priestess, are the icons of a people asked to believe that woman will deify flesh.

Saint Foy enthroned (left and right), Carolingian art, 983-1013. Conques, Church

Virgin of Montserrat (centre), 12th Century. Barcelona, Monastery of Montserrat

Myths and mysteries

Married woman, consecrated woman

Eleanor of Aquitaine (1122-1204) knew all about the three lusts: for power, knowledge and pleasure. Queen of France at fifteen, she separated from her husband Louis VII because of consanguinity and was remarried to Henry II, King of England, holding power jointly with him from the Pyrenees to Scotland. At her side she had a dazzling court which made her into the queen of the troubadours. The mother of ten children, she succeeded in installing her granddaughter, Blanche of Castile, on the throne of France. But, deceived and deserted, she soon discovered the poisons of power. She instigated the revolt of her sons against her husband Henry, who imprisoned her. She believed she had triumphed when her favourite son, Richard the Lionheart, became king. But, stupidly killed, he left the throne to her last born son, the perverse, puny John the Landless, who lost everything. Three weeks before her death, she knew that with the fall of Château Gaillard the immense empire which she had built up was crumbling. The possessive mother found herself, without kingdom or children, at Fontevrault where she had often stayed after 1152. As abbess of this double monastery she was in charge of women as well as men, following the command that Mary received from Christ on the cross, concerning John the apostle: 'Woman, here is your son.' Eleanor loved this prophetic feminine authority of a spiritual mother of all men. A lady who was admired, an experienced mother, now converted to religious life, under her nun's veil she reads her book of devotions: 'Remember not the sins of my youth, nor my transgressions: according to thy mercy remember thou me for thy goodness' sake, O Lord.'[2]

Eleanor of Aquitaine,
Queen of England,
tombstone of the
Platagenets,
13th Century.
Fontevrault Abbey

Mary Magdalene

Medieval piety made Mary Magdalene the most popular saint in history. But it was at the cost of mistaking three New Testament figures for one: Mary of Magdala, whom Jesus had exorcised, the unknown prostitute who bathed the feet of Jesus in tears and perfume, then wiped them away with her hair, and Mary of Bethany who did the same. And the story of Mary the Egyptian, who expiated her sins in the desert for forty-seven years can be added to these. Mary Magdalene thus completes a rehabilitation of the female sinner, the anti-Agnes, as portrayed here by Erhart around 1510. While Agnes hides her untouched body with her hair, Magdalene shows her body restored to wholeness with her hair hanging loose. Her body is in fact a treasure-chest: the back opens to reveal a reliquary. Agnes is the eldest daughter, pure virtue, while Magdalene is the prodigal daughter, virtue recovered. Whereas Donatello could only represent a woman with her body hidden, weathered and wizened, Erhart chose to show a young and firm beauty whose modesty is expressed by her hands being joined in prayer and her head bowed. Magdalene has rediscovered her innocence, that is to say her inability to do harm. In contrast to the pagan nude, the Christian nude does not need to be veiled, except by an uplifting gesture. Magdalene does not fear the effects she might have, nor the looks she attracts. Someone is with her. Did she not say, before recognizing the resurrected Christ, the cherished master: 'He is the gardener'?

Mary Magdalene, carved wood, by Gregor Erhart, c. 1510. Paris, Louvre

Myths and mysteries

Powers

Helena and Theodora represent the antithesis of two feminine powers. One is venerated like a saint, but is not given any particular characteristic on this coin, while the other, who was far from being venerated, has her head surrounded by a halo, a sort of canonization of the Byzantine Empire. Helena, a maidservant at an inn and concubine of Constantius I, was repudiated in favour of a political alliance. In 326, her son the Emperor Constantine, named her Augusta. To gain pardon for ordering the deaths of his bastard son Crispus and his wife Fausta, he ordered Helena to make a pilgrimage to the Holy Places, where she had the Holy Sepulchre completed. Helena is thus the mother restorer and, as the inscription on the coin states, 'Salvation of the State'.

Theodora, the daughter of a circus bear-leader, actress, dancer and prostitute, was an adventurer who achieved everything she wanted. She had the law which classed her among the 'infamous persons' abolished, and was able to marry Emperor Justinian, who was seventeen years her senior. Here she is portrayed at the peak of her glory, in 547, her head adorned with a diadem of pendants, dressed in her scarlet imperial robe. She demanded of the senators that they prostrate themselves to kiss her feet. In 532, seeing her husband give way in the face of a revolt in Constantinople, she pressed him to resist and had thirty thousand people massacred in the circus. 'I love the maxim which says that scarlet makes a beautiful shroud,' she said to him. To die in scarlet or to live in blood?

Theodora surrounded by her court (left), detail, 6th-Century mosaic. Ravenna, Saint Vital Basilica

The Empress Helen (front and back), gold medal, 4th Century. Paris, Bibliothèque Nationale

Myths and mysteries

Bust of Vibia Matidia (left) marble, 90-100. Rome, Capitoline Museum

Sarcophagus of Larthia Seianti (right), Etruscan art. Florence, Archaeological Museum

Beauty

For the people of ancient times, feminine beauty was already something to be questioned. On this Etruscan tomb a young wife is raising the wedding veil from her forehead while, in her left hand, she holds the hard wheatcake of the wedding ceremony. Hanging round her neck is the god of love. Her belt, with the ritual knot, was probably never untied. Although she adopts the pose of a woman longing for life, she has been stiffened by death, her promise unfulfilled. This purely facial beauty is achieved in an even better form in the face of Vibia Matidia, the niece of the Emperor Trajan. Another kind of veil, her hair, is cleverly piled up in a style which balances her features and counterbalances the slenderness of her neck. Why was there a desire to immortalize an ephemeral fashion in marble, in this way? It was through Matidia that the right to inherit the empire was passed to Hadrian. What is more, she was deified in 119 on her death. So the contemporaries of these two women wanted their beauty, a gift from the gods, to be captured at a unique moment of their lives, so that they would always remain alive in our eyes. Their grave expressions with no seductive smile, were intended to set them apart from history and make us question the apparent fragility of their beauty. Through provoking the wonder of the moment, they laid claim to eternity.

SOCIETY
DEPICTED

THE MIDDLE AGES

Chiara Frugoni

This short sketch accompanies brief marginal commentaries to a dossier of illustrations on the theme of women in the Middle Ages, chosen for their meaning. I find it impossible to avoid reminding the reader that every portrait of a woman, whether saint, queen or any other woman, was created at that time in a man's world, or more exactly was created in response to a man's request. Consequently, we find reproduced here, as elsewhere, two types of perspective. On the one hand there is the relationship that unites man and woman, a very rich and very varied relationship, since it embraces the whole spectrum of feelings, from passionate love, tender affection, or yearning of one who pursues and courts a woman as a distant object of desire, through to the feelings of open opposition which we now call misogyny. On the other hand, there is a whole range of feelings centred on the woman's role in the family: these are the numerous expressions of maternal affection seen in hundreds of images of the Virgin and Child, images capable of spanning every degree of tenderness, nurturing and also anxiety, where the colours associated with melancholy become an omen of crucifixion and future death.

It goes without saying that the obsessive repetition of the mother and son theme has for centuries sustained the idea that women have a maternal vocation. Out of the infinite series of images illustrating this theme, there emerges from time to time the duty of procreation, as it was imposed on Eve by the Bible, for example: ' In sorrow thou shalt bring forth children; and thy desire shall be to thy husband and he shall rule over thee' (Genesis 3:16) It is only in the scenes representing the actual moment of birth (for example in the Birth of the Virgin or the Birth of John, fruit of the late fecundity of Elizabeth and Zachariah) that the harshness of the sentence is eased and a space is found for women to express affectionate mutual support: the female figures form a circle around the bed of the new mother, they prepare the linen and poke the fire; one or the other takes the child in her arms. Perhaps because of this ancient and marginalized solidarity, the two great protagonists Eve and Mary are represented side by side on the bronze doors of Hildesheim Cathedral (1015), contradicting an opposition which, as we shall see, was

Society depicted

institutionalized and significant. One side of the double door is dedicated to each of them, as if to illuminate the joint mystery of their story. One important way in which images of women were exploited was in their use to express all those emotions which historically are forbidden to man: desperation, tenderness, fatigue, fear, modesty, laughter. The social code did not allow man to lose control of himself, but on the faces of women those buried feelings could take on form and expression. In the cloister, however, where sisters led their lives protected by their removal from the world, they could leave their own lasting testimony. Some sisters wrote books, others copied them or illustrated them with miniatures, working with complete autonomy, as can sometimes be seen in the explicit language of so many volumes of manuscript. As well as creative work, all kinds of charitable activities took place in the monastery, giving women the right to create their own totally autonomous image.

Preceding pages

Creation of Eve, detail from the Gate of Paradise by Lorenzo Ghiberti, 1425-1452. Florence, Baptistry

Wise virgin from south portal of the western façade of Strasbourg Cathedral, 1230. Strasbourg, Museum of the Works of Notre-Dame

Allegory of Good
Government
*(detail), fresco by
Ambrogio Lorenzetti,
1337 to 1343.
Siena, Palazzo Pubblico,
Room of Peace*

Good and Bad Government

Between 1338 and 1339 Ambrogio Lorenzetti painted a
fresco in a room of the Palazzo Pubblico in Siena on
the orders of the Nine who were governing the city at
that time. The subject was Good and Bad Government
and the effects of each. We have chosen images from
this work because they offer a kind of snapshot, from
the hand of a single painter, of a wide range of women,
from allegorical figures of vices and virtues to real
women of flesh and blood, at work and at leisure.

On the narrowest wall of the room, opposite the big
window, the best form of government is represented.
High up, Wisdom is holding a large set of scales;
underneath, Justice looks up at her, keeping the pans of
the scales balanced and holding two ropes, which
Concord takes up again further down. Concord's
gesture is significant, because concord is the central
theme of the ideological propaganda which the work is
charged to spread. The rope does not finish there; it

holds together twenty-four figures, representing the upper professional classes, bankers, merchants and warriors, and ends up in the noble hands of a grand old man, the Common Good, dressed in white and black, the colours of the Balzana of Siena; he sits enthroned above the Roman she-wolf, an eloquent symbol of the city. Good Government is aided in the sky by the three theological virtues (Faith, Hope and Charity), and is surrounded by the four cardinal virtues: Justice,

Strength, Prudence and Temperance, themselves accompanied by the new virtues of Magnanimity and Peace. Immediately below, soldiers represent the sorry reality of urban government: soldiers everywhere, on foot and on horseback, escort prisoners while two lords, 'of their own free will' as the texts put it, submit by making an offering in the symbolic form of their castles.

Society depicted

—

The adjacent wall shows the town of Siena with all its beautiful palaces and the varied activities of its inhabitants overflowing beyond the walls; the security desired by those in power reigns. Once again real people, peasants and nobles, work or amuse themselves. On the opposite wall, in contrast, there is Bad Government and its effects. The city, already invaded and devastated by war and violence, is in ruins and on fire, populated with corpses. In the countryside, which has been overrun by fighting soldiers, the villages are burning. In Good Government, the Virtues are parading past: all the women are of uncommon beauty and they are richly dressed. Here, even Prudence is shown as unusually youthful: the customary iconography makes her mature. The new figure, Peace, stands out among the Virtues: very beautiful, she's dressed in white and crowned with olive leaves. Peace tramples underfoot a pile of weapons. Her body shows through her diaphanous robes and we can imagine the loving care exciting the painter to draw the points of her breasts with such quasi-classical frankness. We know the artist admired the ancient masterpieces and Ghiberti recounts the accidental discovery in Siena of a naked Venus bearing the inscription 'Lysippus'; he saw her next 'drawn by the hand of one of the city of Siena's really great painters, who was called Ambrogio Lorenzetti'. This statue was later placed in the public square and for the citizens it became a cult object, but it was also held responsible for the successive military defeats suffered by the Republic. Yet again the feminine virtue of beauty becomes an object of suspicion.

Allegory of Bad
Government
*(details: Avarice, Pride,
Vanity), fresco by Ambrogio
Lorenzetti. Siena, Palazzo
Pubblico, Room of Peace*

Society depicted

VANE GLORIA.

Note the new tendency to appreciate the body for its own sake; we find it again in the winged Securitas, who flies naked over the countryside.

In Bad Government on the other hand, the features of the whore of Babylon who represents Tyranny are diabolical. She is accompanied at the head of the procession by Avarice, Pride and Vanity and is advised by Cruelty, Betrayal, Fraud, Fury, Division and War. At her feet the scales of Justice lie broken. They are all figures of women: but it must be admitted that this choice was imposed by the nouns denoting the

qualities, which are all of the feminine gender. The only male name in the chorus of the terrible furies is Furor, Rage, but the painter (or the person supervising the programme of the cycle for him) wanted it represented in the form of a minotaur, the Dantesque symbol of rage; thus no male figure suffers the dishonour of sitting on the terrible bench. The burden of horror which weighs on the women overall does not prevent the painter from attributing distinctive characteristics to each of his figures. Look at the kind of inverted trinity which floats above Bad Government – in the place which the theological virtues occupy above Good; Pride and Vanity, the couple absorbed by a concern for

Allegory of Good Government in the town *(details)*

Society depicted

—
77

themselves always perceived as feminine, still have fine and luminous features. Avarice, on the other hand, performing an activity which was more the privilege of the masculine sex, takes on the appearance of a grasping and repellent old woman. The painter has not flinched from depicting the worst acts of violence: rape is perpetrated in fields by the army rabble. In town – we are coming back to the opposite wall – the peasants are portrayed in a realistic manner, carrying the fruits of their labour, a chicken or a basket on their heads; one

woman is even carrying out hard labouring work alongside the masons, in a scene of neo-realist flavour. All are smaller than the noble women, who spend their time amusing themselves and taking strolls. The circle of young girls drawn by music and rhythm offers another allegory of concord which the government of Nine is supposed to establish. The choice of eminent women representing the privileged class, suitably tall and slender, evidently did not happen by chance. The milieu in which the young girl who is going to be married

moves on horseback does not seem very different; she resembles a small queen who is being led to her husband by her companions in the celebration. This interpretation is confirmed by the astute observation of Bernadin of Siena, who in 1425 commented on the fresco as follows: 'I see sowing, bathing, riding, I see young girls going to be married, I see flocks of sheep, etc.' Another beautiful woman is the 'lady with the small dogs', who is heading for the countryside with the hunters.

Allegory of Good
Government in the
countryside
(detail, left)

Allegory of Good
Government in the town
(detail, right)

Society depicted

The Court of Love
(left), relief in ivory, early
14th Century. Florence,
Museum of Bargello

The Kiss (right), courtly
scene, 14th-Century fresco.
Avignon, Museum of the
Petit Palais

A man's view
Courtly love

On the walls of Bad Government, we can already see that the mirror, a feminine attribute *par excellence*, permits Vanity to see her own beauty and finery in spite of the leaden skies under which she is forced to evolve. It is an ivory mirror, carved on the back like the one shown opposite. The scene denotes that the meticulous preparations, for which the mirror is the essential tool, are merely a prelude to the erotic encounter – a simplistic reading, certainly, but inescapable. The episode almost always takes place in an idyllic atmosphere: either in the untamed forest, perfect for long walks, or in the garden, an enclosed space created by man to provide the ideal setting for human pleasure.

Since the mirror, like so many other objects, is made by the hand of man, masculine superiority as usual marks the psychological motivation behind these superb products of the applied arts. The woman yields and the man controls the events in the amorous chase. In fact in the *Roman de la Rose*, the very long allegory of the rose which is to be plucked and carried off, the god of Love dictates his laws to the courageous knight: 'He who wishes to take Love for his master must be courteous and without pride, elegant and joyous and valued for his generosity'. The tale is thus given the characteristics of a chivalrous hunt which in reality is a cynical pursuit, ending in mere copulation. The rose heroine becomes a simple lady or more exactly a human being of the female sex. In the ivory, the knight in the countryside leaves his horse with his squire and barely touches his lady in his most courtly wooing. In the other scene, set in the house said to be Queen Jeanne's, the approach is so far advanced that the dove seems like a warning *et incarnatus est* – a quasi-blasphemous evocation.

Society depicted

—

Seduction

On the part of the ecclesiastical hierarchy in commissions of a specifically religious nature, the conception of woman hardly changes, keeping her seductive qualities in the foreground. The great archetype is the body of Eve who, while she could not resist the serpent, succeeded in making herself irresistible to her mate. The famous relief in Autun Cathedral (12th century) takes the successive phases of this history of damnation almost to the bounds of probability. Eve, lying languorously on her side, picks the forbidden fruit and at the same time, without waiting for a single moment to pass, turns to Adam to seduce him, while a branch of the fig tree conveniently spreads its young leaves to cover the intimate parts of a body which has already lost its innocence. The carving from the synagogue in Strasbourg is no less ambiguous; without doubt she represents conquered Faith, but defeat does not deprive her of any of her gentle attraction.

*The Temptation of Eve
(left), relief attributed to
Gislebertus, lintal of the
north portal of the
cathedral, 12th Century.
Autun, Rolin Museum*

*The Synagogue (right),
Alsatian school, 13th
Century. Strasbourg,
Museum of the Works of
Notre-Dame*

Society depicted

Profane intimacy

When we leave the walls of churches for those of private houses, we find expression becoming more frank. In Ferrara at the Palazzo Schifanoia, the illustration of the amorous delinquencies of Venus and Mars shows at the side of the bed the weapons of the conquered warrior and the pomegranate of the goddess. In Saluzzo at the castle of Mantua, the old men throw themselves into the Fountain of Youth and are suddenly young and sprightly, ready to roam the woods – these same secret woods which cover the ivory mirrors – *'dedans cest boys vous faut venir pour nostres amours nius acuplir'* ('You must enter these woods if you wish our love to be consumated.')

The Fountain of Youth *(detail, left) fresco, late 14th Century-early 15th Century. Castle of Mantua*

The love of the God Mars and the nymph Ylia *(right) fresco, Francesco del Cossa, 1476. Ferrara, Schifanoia Palace*

Society depicted

—

The Triumph of Death
*(detail, left), Siena fresco,
14th Century. Subiaco,
monastery of Saint Benoit
called Sacro Speco*

Misogynies

Now we come to the extremes of misogyny: since women are customarily treated with contempt, Death itself becomes spontaneously identified with a feminine figure. We are spoilt for choice among numerous images. In Subiaco each time the monks descended to the cemetery they had to look at the fresco representing Death on horseback, a decomposing skeleton, who nevertheless still has evident female attributes, drooping breasts and long hair. Remember here the flowing locks of Eve in Autun, finery worthy of the sirens. Death pays no attention to the poor souls pleading with her on her left, but she stabs directly at the noble hunters and condemns them to confirm tragically the proverb: 'They went to play, and were themselves played with'. We

would also be tempted to interpret a certain scorn for the feminine condition in the miniaturized portrayal of Eve's head which the eternal Father extracts from Adam's ribs on the fresco in the Church of San Biagio in Caserta in Campania; the painter, slavishly following the words of Genesis, has stuck the minuscule face on to Adam's emaciated side.

The Creation of Eve (right), Gothic fresco, mid-15th Century. Piedimonte Matese, Church of Saint Biago

Society depicted

The same misogyny makes the figure of woman the incarnation of rage and immoderate passion. Choir-stalls frequently present the theme of the wife beating her husband, probably the reverse of what happened in reality! *Rage*, by Giotto, in the Cappella degli Scrovegni in Padua, bares her breasts and turns against herself the aggressiveness she cannot display towards others; thus she commits a second sin, of immodesty. The old blond Avarice by Dürer in the Kunsthistorisches Museum in Vienna also reveals her breast, and here we might recall the bad trinity by Lorenzetti on the fresco in Siena. Related Vanity is the young woman attending to her hair in front of a mirror held by the devil disguised as a chambermaid in Hieronymus Bosch's famous work, *The Seven Deadly Sins*. She represents Pride here. This scene is astonishingly close to a morality written by the Augustine Brother Filippo of the Agazzari (Siena, *c*.1339-1422). It is the story of a very beautiful woman, whose husband was madly in love with her and 'who was having her face made up by the devil whom she had taken for a chambermaid'; when her real servant arrives, she finds the face of her mistress dreadfully blackened. The lady tries to wash herself, but evidently she does not manage to clean from her cheeks the blackness of sin which the devil has smeared her with. Terror, despair ... laid down on her bed, the woman dies and decomposes immediately. This fable certainly serves to interpret in edifying terms the sudden death of a particularly beautiful woman, and not without a strong misogynist emphasis.

Rage *(left)*, Allegory of Virtues and Vices *(detail), Giotto, early 14th Century. Padua, Chapel of the Scrovegni*

Pride *(right) one of* The Seven Deadly Sins, *Hieronymus Bosch, late 15th Century. Madrid, Prado*

superbia

Private emotions
Pain

Let us move on to the hidden area already mentioned: that spectrum of feelings forbidden to men but permissible for women. The portal of Paradise at Magdeburg Cathedral shows on the faces of the Foolish Virgins a precise typology of tears; the same tears are furrowed into the features of Martha weeping for Lazarus her dead brother, and also those of so many Madonnas at the foot of the cross, or so many Magdalenes. One could believe that Grünewald's Magdalene is going to break her fingers under the weight of despair and I would also like to recall Masaccio's at the Neapolitan Museum of Capodimonte, an unforgettable image in a red cloak, her arms raised like the branches of a tree, adorned as ever with Eve's long hair. Suffering, maternal pain this time, even becomes an expression of the masses in portrayals of the Massacre of the Innocents.

Saint Martha in tears (left), fragment from the tomb of Saint Lazarus, sculpture by Martin called the Monk, 12th Century. Autun, Rolin Museum

Mary Magdalene at the foot of the Cross (right), detail from the Issenheim Altarpiece by Mathias Grünewald, 1512-10. Colmar, Museum of Unterlinden

Modesty

But we are not invariably confronted with such
dramatic extremes. In artistic works, images of woman
also embody delicate nuances such as modesty: this
feeling can clearly be read in the melancholy eyes of
the Virgin in the *Annunciation with Saint Margaret
and Saint Asano* by Simone Martini at the Uffizi in
Florence (1333). The moment is that where she recoils,
creating a vertiginous void between her and the angel,
clasping her mantle to her breast in a movement which
is the exact reverse of the impudent movement made
by Rage in the chapel of the Scrovegni. This gesture
reappears in the great work by an anonymous master,
in the north choir of Naumburg Cathedral (*c*.1255): the
wife of the Margrave Ekkehart, the very noble and
discreet Uta, clutching one edge of her cloak with her
right hand while raising the other edge with her left.

These gestures convey a precise psychological state,
in contrast to the conventional, four-square
stance of her husband.

*The Margrave Uta (left),
the Master of Naumburg,
1250-1260. Naumburg
Cathedral, choir of the
Founders*

Annunciation with Saint
Margaret and Saint Asano
*(detail, right)
Simone Martini, 1333.
Florence, Uffizi*

Society depicted

The Month of August *(left)* *fresco of* The Work of the Month, *early 15th Century. Trente, Château de Bon Counseil*

Head of the Virgin (?) from the Ancient Abbey Notre-Dame at Issoudun, 12th Century. Issoudun, Saint Roch Museum

Fatigue

With his extraordinary talent for facial expression, the Master of Naumburg (see preceding page) was able to depict the wild bitterness of a woman with the features of an old servant in the episode of Peter's Renunciation, a striking contrast to the Margravine Uta, who evolves in a completely different world. Elsewhere servants are also represented, in interior scenes such as Anne and Elizabeth giving birth, or like this woman (a Virgin?), from the ancient Abbey of Issoudun, probably lying by a new-born baby, resting on her hand. Outside the house, serving women work in the fields with the men. For example on the walls of the Château de Bon Conseil in Trente – only one example from a wealth of material – in a very animated episode showing the harvest, the women reapers are in the foreground, bent double and well-covered, in spite of the scorching August sun, to respect the demands of modesty.

Society depicted

Role reversal

The reversal of roles, in relation to an ancient ideology, is especially apparent in this strange Saint Joseph, who during the Nativity is poking the fire without – for reasons that are easy to understand – concerning himself with taking on his role of father.

War is supposed to be uniquely and exclusively masculine, the theatre of violence and strength, but certain images show how important women's assistance was. On a miniature representing the encampment of the Crusaders under the walls of Jerusalem, a group of women and children with their buckets in their hands are busy grubbing a living for their families.

The Nativity (left) detail from an altarpiece, Konrad von Soest, late 14th Century. Bad Wildungen, Church

The Siege of Jerusalem (detail, right) 15th-Century miniature. Paris, Bibliothèque Nationale

Society depicted

—

Powers
Almost queens

Our journey finishes with Agnes Sorel, favourite of Charles VII, in the château at Loches. That expression is unforgettable, in spite of her lowered eyes attempting to compensate for the immodesty of her naked breast. Her bodice is unlaced, surely to show the charms which enslaved the king up to her death, but also to evoke the birth of her daughters, Marie, Charlotte and Jeanne. Neither her lowered eyes nor the devotional book which she is holding succeed in distracting us from her attractions. This work is a copy, carried out by an unknown painter, and we receive the same impression from the 'original', the *Virgin and Child* which Jean Fouquet painted, taking the king's mistress for his model. Her uncovered breast is of great beauty, much more realistic than the other pious images of the *Virgo lactans*. Clearly the ermine and crown evoke a queen. Agnes on her deathbed was also represented by Jacques Morel (?) with the features of a modest young girl, her hands joined, watched over by the angels: 'Life withdrawing was beginning to take with it the disillusions of life. A smile seemed to sit on her lips... Like the sculptor of the Middle Ages, inlaying her to rest on this funeral bed, death had given her the appearance of a young girl' (Marcel Proust).

The features of Agnes Sorel used for The Virgin and Child *(left), Jean Fouquet, 15th Century. Anvers, Royal Museum of Fine Art*

Agnes Sorel *(right) in the style of Jean Fouquet, 15th Century. Loches, Château*

Beauty
The beautiful saint

'See how the saints are depicted on the paintings shown to you, so that, seeing such a noble and beautiful girl, you may find joy, strength and safety in her and banish doubt from your minds.' Thus preached Giordano of Pisa on 22 November 1303, expressing a convention which always surprises us when we visit churches peopled with such noble and beautiful figures, gorgeously dressed. Confirmation that this was a requirement is to be seen in the figure of Saint Margaret by Piero Lorenzetti, in which the figure's very elegant garment is gaping open under the weight of bright golden buttons; or in that of Catherine of Alexandria by Simone Martini, where the brilliance of the cloak appears to symbolize the splendours to which queens must become accustomed; or indeed in this figure by the Master of Saint Sebastian, Josse Lieferinxe. Even in real life, saints had difficulties because of their physical appearance. Catherine of Siena (1347-80) was initially rejected by the Dominican nuns of the town. According to her biographer, Raymond of Capua, the nuns said: 'if she was too beautiful we should be afraid of causing some scandal, because of the evil nature of the times'. A timely illness disfigured her and her shoulders were draped with the habit of the third order nuns of Penitence. Margaret of Cortona, too, was very beautiful; she wanted to mutilate herself by cutting off her nose and lips, when doing penance following the violent death of her lover. Her confessor forbade her, for fear of infection and death. In fact he could see in such a desire an inclination to suicide (killing her body to rid herself of cumbersome beauty), and he feared she might be thought a leper: leprosy ate away at the nose and would have betrayed the presence of sexual guilt. All signs of decomposition had to be forcefully denied, for they would have contradicted that virginal integrity which, sadly lost, was still spiritually preserved.

Saint Catherine, *The Master of Saint Sebastian,*
Josse Lieferinxe, School of Avignon , 1493-1508.
Avignon, Petit-Palais Museum

FROM THE SKY
TO THE EARTH

6TH-18TH CENTURIES

Joël Cornette

n the France of the 'Century of Saints', Pierre de Bérulle, one of the authors of Catholic reform, wrote that 'the greatest motive cometh not from heaven'. From the Renaissance to the Age of Enlightenment, when Europe was in ferment with great discoveries and with the two great reforms, of absolute monarchy and of mercantile ascendancy, men set themselves to master and take possession of the world and of a Nature which they perceived as 'written in mathematical language' (Galileo).

This work of conquest and objectivity also affected the world of art and, particularly in the prosperous Holland of the *burghers*, which had inherited the imitative pictorial traditions of the Flemish primitives, imposed a representation of what the eye, and the eye alone, can see: the tangible nature of the world, as perceived visually, which the painter or engraver is able to fix on the canvas, wood or copper.

In this major revolution which consisted in taking possession of the world, materially and intellectually, did the representation of woman become more realistic, more earthly? Humanism and the Renaissance, which were above all a dazzling rediscovery of antiquity, no doubt contributed to the discovery in her of a body and a desire unmindful of the curse of Original Sin. But the prudish and moralizing vigilance of the Churches, both Catholic and Protestant, quickly clothed her again and hid the breasts that they did not wish to see: woman, painted, drawn and engraved almost always by men, became a more integral part of her social environment than ever before. She was woman idealized and allegorized by painters of the princely courts, woman reduced to her social and domestic roles and functions by the men of the increasingly bourgeois societies. In all cases, or nearly all, she was confined to the place to which the massed ranks of the male powers and canons of thought wished to assign her. And even if she could be presented as the holder of a power, sovereign or witch, she was more often the Other, the Shadowy Threat, brutally displaying (as with the stream of naked corpses that seem to spring from the body of Catherine de Medicis, the black queen, on that sinister Saint Bartholomew's Day: see page 116) the only power that no man has ever had, that of giving birth.

Preceding pages

The Garden of Earthly Delights *(altarpiece), Hieronymus Bosch, early 16th Century. Madrid, Prado*

From the sky to the earth

—

Let us, then, step cautiously into this everyday world, this intimate space. In the painting opposite, woman's presence is felt through the broom, the large duster, the things that are scrubbed, washed, polished. Two wide-flung doors and a set of keys left in the door are signs of welcome. But make no mistake: before crossing the threshold of this domestic paradise criss-crossed with rays of light projected on to the ground like protective curtains, one must demonstrate allegiance by swapping one's outdoor shoes for slippers. The housewife has left them there, like a final barrier to the entrance of her territory, which is also that of her private life. Painted by Samuel van Hoogstraten, these meticulous gestures of order and cleanliness are not simply an objective and rational rendering; they cannot be understood without reference to family life in the Dutch towns of the 17th century and to some of the significance attributed to it. For devout Calvinists, the representation of the household, the guarantor of domestic and biblical order and simplicity, reflects the image of a pacified state and society which has driven into the shadows all traces of savagery and violence. The house, the family, the heroic housewife constantly struggling against dirt and disorder, are transformed into models for the perfect republic in miniature, of which they constitute the womb and the reflection.

Interior: the slippers,
*Samuel van Hoogstraten,
17th Century.*
Paris, Louvre

From the sky to the earth

Virgins
From the empress virgin...

A soul first, then a woman. A majestic Virgin with a stony gaze, to which one is forced to raise one's eyes. Ensconced in her is the Infant, Christ and King. The heavenly and terrestrial hierarchies merge. Giotto also leads us into the kingdom of Heaven, of which that of Earth is a pale reflection. In this Italy of the early Renaissance, a crossroads of Byzantine, Greek, Roman and Gothic influences, the painter has placed a woman's body and flesh. A knee, a bust, a hand holding back the Infant. A woman is here, monumental and seated. We see birds in a cloudless sky, and urban palaces; the town has replaced the angels. In the Florence of the Medicis, blessed by the graces of neo-platonism and the dreams of Marsilio Ficino, the *Virgin and Child* by Botticelli attempts to depict the humanists' impossible ambition: to reconcile the Christian world and the natural world, the intelligible and the perceptible.

From left to right:
Virgin and Child, *mosaic,*
6th Century. Ravenna,
San Appolinare in Classe
Virgin and Child
Enthroned, *Giotto, late 13th*
Century. Florence, Uffizi
Virgin and Child, *Sandro*
Botticelli, 15th Century.
Turin, Sabanda Gallery

From the sky to the earth

... to rapturous maternity

Idealization, the refinement of the body's substance, a reflection of the Inaccessible through line and drawing: the sublimated form of an impossibly perfect woman refers the carnal envelope back to its spiritual essence, to the pure idea of which she is no more than a reflection. Beauty and love, physical attractions, may constitute an initiation into the world beyond, mad temptation, a crazy attempt by men to approach God. The *Madonna di Loreto*, or 'Virgin with Pilgrims', commissioned on the occasion of the 1600 papal jubilee for the altar of San Agostino Church, Rome, was, it is said, strongly criticized. What was the purpose in showing dirty feet and torn clothing, why precisely were these two poor pilgrims, on their knees, crippled

with fatigue, chosen from among the cohorts of seekers after God, led by the irresistible hunger for divine things? The answer is that in this city, where anything can happen, where the supernatural is to be found rubbing shoulders with the day-to-day, miracles are always possible, and the Virgin herself, like a tall and wonderful living statue straight from Greek or Roman antiquity, can come out on the step of a humble door to present the blessed God Child to the pilgrims, offering the simplest of his human creatures the most beautiful of promises and a spiritual compensation for misfortune, misery and oppression.

With Rembrandt, the divine becomes indistinguishable from the day-to-day. Here we have

From the sky to the earth

detailed observation of the familiar and the domestic, of quietness, intimacy, maternal tenderness, calm, and of the tactile evidence of beings and objects. The halo has gone; Mary mother of Jesus passes her days in happiness, cradling her new-born child; her spouse, in shadow, is going about his ordinary business. Without this mysterious light emanating from the faces and bodies, without this strange device which transforms the painting into a theatrical stage, without this great red curtain, which seems to signify to us that the divine, so close but inaccessible, has become incarnated in the most humble and humane of existences, would we know that this scene was not completely ordinary?

The Madonna di Loreto or 'Virgin with Pilgrims' (left), Caravaggio, late 16th Century. Rome, San Agostino

The Holy Family or The Woodcutter's Family (right), Rembrandt, 1646. Kassel, Gemäldegalerie

From the sky to the earth

Forms of ecstasy
Teresa and God's wound

'The transports of which I speak are completely different from these flights of tender devotion... From time to time a spear is plunged in and penetrates into the very centre of one's entrails, piercing one's heart... No language can express nor exalt the manner in which God gives one this wound, and the torment He produces... Your Love, penetrating every part of my being, plunged me into an agony so sweet that my soul would have wished never to emerge from it... While I was in this state, I could see close to me, on my left, an angel in bodily form... It was not large, but small and extremely beautiful; from its fiery face it appeared to be one of the most high among those who seem completely consumed with love...

    I could see the angel holding a long golden spear in its hand, the iron end of which, I think, gave off a small flame. It seemed to plunge it repeatedly through my heart, pushing it as far as my entrails. When it withdrew it, it seemed as though this fire removed them with it and left me utterly aflame with an immense love of God. The pain was so sharp that it made me groan in the manner of which I have spoken. But the sweetness caused by this incomparable torment is so overwhelming that one's soul cannot wish for it to end, nor be satisfied with anything that is not God. It is not a physical but a spiritual torment, although one's body cannot help sharing in it to some extent and even to a great degree...

    During the days this fervour lasted, I felt beside myself. I should have liked to see nothing and say nothing, but simply to bask in my torment; for to me it was a glory above all other glories here below.'

Terese d'Àvila, *The Book of Life*

The Ecstasy of Saint Teresa, *sculpture by Gian Lorenzo Bernini, 1644-1651. Rome, Santa Maria della Vittoria*

Ardour and rapture

The controlled sensuality of Canova, seeking to express the state of grace and innocence of a first embrace, contrasts with flattering ardour in the shadowy warmth of a boudoir. Caught up in a hot-blooded game of love, two ardent creatures, young and beautiful, breathing, alive, are smiling, entangled by passion and weakness. Transported by a feverish rapture, they burn with an unnameable desire, completely carried away.
Like Greuze and Chardin, Fragonard reinvented in his own fashion a world which neutralizes and ignores the presence of the spectator, a world of vibrant intensity, transmitted through the caress of light and paint, translating rapture and ecstasy, allowing us to see

Two young breasts joining and palpitating together,
Two twenty-year-old mouths united in the same fire,
Mingling their delicious labour and their languorous cries,
Their greedy kisses, moist and sweet,

André Chénier[1]

But are we so far from the Proscribed? On a table, on the left of the painting, in the foreground, the painter has placed an apple clearly on display. It is lit by the great diagonal of light which gently plays over the bodies.

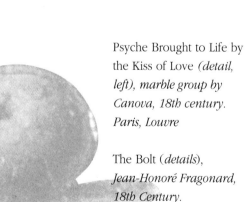

Psyche Brought to Life by the Kiss of Love *(detail, left), marble group by Canova, 18th century. Paris, Louvre*

The Bolt (*details*), *Jean-Honoré Fragonard, 18th Century. Paris, Louvre*

From the sky to the earth

—

113

Queens
The hive of political intrigue

A woman in mourning is seated close to an empty
throne: Catherine de Medicis, widow of Henry II,
assumes the regency during the minority of her son
Charles IX. Around the black queen, like a busy hive,
spreading its splendours in a place of fragile peace, the
festive court revolves slowly in an interplay of glances
and ostentation. Dance steps are sketched to the
discreet music of flutes, lyres and viols. To receive the
ambassadors from distant Poland, Catherine has laid out
the pomp and finery of a well-ordered society:
superficial pleasures of a temporary paradise in a large,
luxuriant garden, closed in by hedges and balustrades.
This world of prodigality, decorum and appearance is
reserved, as Rabelais said of his Thélème Monastery, for
'high-born, well-educated persons, used to decent
company'. No one, it would seem, can trouble this
peaceful moment. Shortly before his coming of age,
Catherine recommended Charles IX to keep his
courtiers 'cheerful and busy at some honest matter in
order to prevent their minds from doing ill'. But can a
woman, even a Regent, constrain human passions? Can
she prevent the swords of the white-ruffed princes from
being drawn from their sheaths? Several months after
this brilliant reception of the Polish ambassadors, the
massacre of Protestants at Wassy would herald the
rumbling of the drums of war, and plunge the kingdom
into more than thirty years of violence and horror.

Catherine de Medicis,
*tapestry by Arazzo di
Valois, 16th Century.
Florence, Uffizi*

From the sky to the earth

Mary the consoler, Catherine the killer

The beliefs, discussions and imagination that work upon an event are often more significant than the reconstitution of a political coherence of which most of the principal participants and witnesses were unaware. Thus, like most of his contemporaries, the painter François Dubois accused Catherine and her son, King Charles IX, seen firing an arquebus from a high window of the Louvre, of unleashing the frenzy of killing which drenched Paris in blood on 24 and 25 August 1572, before spreading to many other cities. This terrible representation of the Catholics' ferocious attacks on the corpses of the Protestants, who are being dragged along, mutilated and decapitated, also depicts an even stronger image. The murderous widow, standing over a pile of naked bodies, as though she had just slaughtered the men as she brought them into the world, is also a reversal of the image of the Virgin Mother with the large cloak, she who welcomes fearful men and women with the promise of salvation. By metamorphosing Mary the consoler into Catherine the killer, the Huguenot painter not only wished to expunge the age-old image of Our Lady the mother, sovereign and divine; the black queen who wealds power in the kingdom of France becomes a monstrous, frozen image of the murderous state.

Saint Bartholomew's Day *(left), François Dubois, 16th Century. Lausanne, Cantonal Museum of the Fine Arts*

Our Lady of Mercy *(right), relief in polychrome stone, around 1420. Yugoslavia, Ptujs, Ka Gora*

From the sky to the earth

Threshold of the home

Strange disorder, strange celebration. Everything revolves around a double centre: the ground glaringly illuminated, the black hole of a well. In a circle around this centre, from the bottom of the town towards the open church, through the Blue Boat tavern, men, women, children seem to be spinning along in an inescapable whirlwind which carries them from Christmas (at the bottom) to Carnival (left hand side of painting), from Carnival to Lent (right hand side of painting).

And, above all, at the back of the square, a solitary house. A woman up a ladder is washing the windows; another, on her knees and in her chemise has taken out all the cooking pots and kitchen utensils – gridirons, pot-hooks – and is scouring them. They are spring cleaning. A man sits at the side of the cross-shaped window, watching the great round of life and death unfolding at his feet. Could he not be a figure of the risen Christ? This image is that of a whole universe, space, time, rich, poor, disorder (left), order and discipline (right), all brought together on a wide public square which has become a grand metaphor for the world.

From the sky to the earth

—

In the teeming anthology of his *Children's Games*, perhaps conceived as a mirror for men's folly, Pieter Bruegel has not forgotten the woman with the broom chasing off the little intruders from the entrance to a large public building. A year after his *The fight between Carnival and Lent*, establishing the woman as the guardian of the thresholds to the permissible and to the forbidden, the painter again showed a public square containing eternal conflict between order and disorder, freedom and obedience, amusement and instruction.

The fight between Carnival and Lent *(detail, left), Pieter Bruegel the Elder, 1559. Vienna, Kunsthistorisches Museum*

Children's Games *(detail, right) Pieter Bruegel the Elder, 1560. Vienna, Kunsthistorisches Museum*

From the sky to the earth

—

Domestic order, collective chaos

The turbulence of the world is pushed back outside the thick walls of a tranquilly opulent house. Here, everything has been disciplined, civilized, everything is clean, spotless, white (or black), and what disorder there is, caused by children playing on the floor, is discreet. Everyone knows his place, in a painting which above all demonstrates social, family and domestic order, but also presents sobriety, frugality, piety, humility, fidelity. *Pater familias*, the head of the household, is seated, enthroned next to his spouse, attentive and loving. She is holding his hand, but is also ready to obey his slightest wish. The numerous children, of all ages, express the everlasting nature of the home, citadel of order and morality, a miniature version of an ideal State. 'The first community', wrote Dr Johan van Beverwijck in 1643, 'is that of marriage itself; thereafter in a family household with children, in which all things are common. That is the first principle of a town and thus the seed of a common State.' Opposite this morally pure home stands the inn, scene of bacchic licence and jovial liberty, of noisy and well-oiled fun, of 'insolence and dissoluteness', as described in the moralizing texts and edicts of the municipalities, of States, and of the Churches. Men and women, well-fleshed, are united in a comforting, confraternal and bawdy sociability. Amsterdam in 1613 boasted no less than 518 taverns; Jan Steen's father was a brewer and he himself kept an inn to supplement his income from painting.

Interior, family group,
Adriaen van Ostade,
17th Century.
Paris, Louvre

Feast at an Inn
(detail, right), Jan
Steen, 17th Century.
Paris, Louvre

From the sky to the earth

—

Rich and poor

Interior with a woman
delousing a child's hair,
Pieter de Hooch,
17th Century. Amsterdam,
Rijksmuseum

In this Holland, which became bourgeois very early on,
it is rare to find visual evidence of inequalities and
exclusions. Here two women are busy with the daily
chore of delousing, a vital practice in a world prone to
the risks of epidemics and of the plague, which can be
carried by a mere flea. The 'culture of the eye' has, in
these two pictures, encouraged the painter to pay
particular attention to day-to-day life. Thanks to his
camera obscura, which projects a reduced image of the
outside world on to a flat surface, he could capture then
reproduce a living vision.

From the sky to the earth

—

122

Compare the discreet opulence of a perfectly kept domestic interior with the poverty of a hovel open to the four winds. Every detail serves to contrast the two irreconcilable worlds, point for point; they reveal the brutality of social relationships when collective and traditional solidarity brakes down in the face of market and monetary forces. During a stay in Amsterdam in the early 1630s, René Descartes wrote to Guez de Balzac that 'in this big city ... everyone is so concerned with his own profit'; one could live there a whole lifetime 'without ever being seen'.

The Grinder's Family,
Gerard Ter Borch,
17th Century. Berlin,
Gemäldegalerie, Staatliche
Museen Preussischer
Kulturbesitz

From the sky to the earth

—

Women in a man's life
Tenderness

From left to right:

The Prophetess Anna *or*
Rembrandt's mother,
Rembrandt, 1631.
Amsterdam, Rijksmuseum

Family Group (*unfinished*),
Rembrandt. Brunswick,
Staatliche Herzog Anton
Ulrich Museum

Hendrickje Stoffels in Bed,
Rembrandt. Edinburgh,
National Gallery

The Jewish Bride,
Rembrandt. Amsterdam,
Rijksmuseum

Here we see collected together some of the women
who presumably knew Rembrandt intimately. That must
be so with his old mother. But this family portrait,
painted a year before his death? Was it motivated by
nostalgia for the happy years with Saskia, whom he
loved so tenderly? This woman who is lifting the
curtain, is she perhaps Hendrickje Stoffels, Titus's wet
nurse and the painter's faithful companion? Who are the
couple in the painting known as The Jewish Bride?
Some people believe it to be Rembrandt's well-loved
son as an adult, just before his marriage.

But it does not matter: from the 'delicate style'
of the first painting to the 'crude style' of the Jewish
Bride, the same love unites these portraits, painted
thirty years apart. The play of glances, of bodies and of
light express an equal tenderness for the beloved
object, whether it be the Book or the She, this 'Jewish
Bride' for example, whose breast is lightly touched by a
tender hand.

From the sky to the earth

Couples

Far from idealism, well beyond any conventional pose and social status underlined by the richness of finery, a woman steps away from a dark wall in the frame of a painting which one could confuse with a window. Her fan is already opening towards us and she seems to be leaning on the frame, in order to leave it, in order to free herself; she seems to call upon us as witnesses, to fix our gaze with hers, so present, so insistent, so staring. Across the centuries Agatha Bas, anxiously questioning, draws us into her world.

Cornelis Anslo, who commissioned this monumental (1.76m x 2.10m) double portrait was a rich Amsterdam draper and shipowner. From 1617 onwards he was also the Mennonite pastor of a community to the north of the capital. Rembrandt shows him at his desk, practising on his wife the sermon he is preparing, paradoxically illustrating what one can neither see nor show: the unique rule of life and faith, the divine message, can only be conveyed by words, and especially not by images. 'The Papists will have their chapels and beautiful paintings, and it seems to them that God is represented well there. But for His part, He repudiated everything. So what must be done? Return to His word' (Calvin). Big Bible open, the word, the hearer, light shed on the hands, the intent faces, and the pages of the Book. Concentrating, listening attentively, under the gaze of her husband, whose words are stirring her deeply, the woman here provides discreet but unquestionably efficient support for an official life to which she has no access.

Surely Rembrandt here goes beyond the usual definition of 'portrait'?

Portrait of Agatha Bas,
Rembrandt, 1641.
London, Royal Collection,
St James's Palace, © Her
Majesty the Queen

From the sky to the earth

Portrait of Cornelis Anslo with his Wife,
Rembrandt, 1641. Berlin, Gemäldegalerie,
Staatliche Museen Preussischer
Kulturbesitz

From the sky to the earth

Rebellions
Dance of the outsiders

The defeated leave few traces in history, and rare indeed are the painters and engravers who have sided with men and women in revolt.

In 1521, Urs Graf drew and engraved proud and robust young women apparently taking their revenge for centuries of servitude: women thrashing a monk, an Amazon astride Aristotle, the symbol of order, authority, hierarchy and knowledge.

A little later, his pen sketches peasants dancing, moving somewhat clumsily, heavy but determined. The man and woman support each other, showing solidarity, strengthened by joint action, wearing the same smile of complicity and of menace. Awaking the earth with their unison stamping, their gazes are converging on the phallic knife, placed in full view. The dance of the poor and the blows which their feet give the earth announce the revolt and the death promised to the powerful. We are in south-west Germany in 1525, at the time of the Peasant's Revolt. Living outside society, roaming the highways and byways of Italy, Switzerland and the Holy Roman Empire, Urs Graf followed and understood the revolt which agricultural workers led against the dictatorship of the lords who owned the land and made the laws; is his signature not pierced by a dagger, the very one which the dancing couple are carrying? But the clay pot and the world upside down have little power faced with the iron pot and the world the right way up. The bloody repression of the revolt in Swabia and Franconia unquestionably caused more than 100,000 deaths, while Martin Luther called upon people to 'obey authority, no matter how tyrannical, how intolerable'.

And whilst he was so joyfully illustrating the overturning of order and of gender, Urs Graf was beating his legal wife so badly that he was sentenced to several terms of imprisonment in the gaols of Basle ...

Celebration and Revolt
*(left), engraving by Urs
Graf, 16th Century. Paris,
Bibliothèque d'Art et
d'Archéologie*

Aristotle *(right) engraving
by Urs Graf. Paris,
Bibliothèque Nationale*

From the sky to the earth

Witches

From the Renaissance to the Enlightenment, tens of thousands of women were persecuted for the crime of witchcraft and devil worship, by men who were also their judges. Between 1580 and 1640 there was an epidemic of witch-burnings. At the centre of the accusations, the spectacle of the sabbath gives legal power and form to the worst of the punishments, because, by liberating the dark forces of unsatisfied desire it also unleashes the power of destruction and death, which the witch has been given by her new and sole master the Devil. Crowning the edifice of offenses was the crime of 'human and divine lese-majesty'; this resulted in the torture and death by burning of those said to have transgressed all the rules, to have subverted the power hierarchy of heaven and earth. Listen to Madeleine des Aymards, a fifteen-year-old servant girl, making a statement to the Criminal Lieutenant General of Riom, in central France, about the sabbath in which she took part for several nights during the year 1606. After she had been lifted up through the chimney on a broom 'and carried off through the air to a mountain, completely naked, just as she was', she found 'a great number of people, men and women, of all classes and types'. Dressed in a black chasuble, the Devil, 'had his robe up around his waist, exposing his naked arse, and each of his assistants went up and kissed his arsehole ...' He then asked them to report on 'the evil deeds they had done, who they had killed, poisoned, or made ill, what livestock they had caused to die.' He then gave the participants powders and ointments to 'call up the evil which they wanted to commit as the whim took them'. The master of the coven extinguished the light, 'and then each of the men helping him took each of the women and girls who were present and laid them on the ground and had their way with them'.

Witches' Sabbath *(left), anonymous watercolour, 17th Century. Paris, Private Collection*

Young Witch and Dragon *(right), Hans Baldung Grien, 1515. Karlsruhe, Staatliche Kunsthalle*

From the sky to the earth

—

130

Women in revolution

Charlotte Corday came from a family of penniless Normandy aristocrats; Marie-Jeanne Philipon was the daughter and granddaughter of Parisian artisans and shopkeepers. Everything seems to place the murderess with the ebony-handled dagger in opposition to the bluestocking baptized by Sainte-Beuve 'the Sévigné of the middle classes'. However, when they were condemned to the guillotine, both were added by the pamphleteers and news vendors to the long list of unnatural female monsters, those who failed to respect the limitations imposed on their sex. One of them dared, on 13 July 1793, the eve of the anniversary of the storming of the Bastille, to assassinate Marat, 'the people's friend', and the other was the mastermind behind those who were later to be called the Girondins. Mme Roland was also accused of being in control of the Ministry of the Interior, in the person of her husband. These two paintings also show the difficulty of producing an image of a woman who does not play the game that men's society has for so long assigned her. The Revolution, after all, did not pull down those internal Bastilles, which were much more sturdy and enduring than the sinister prison of the monarchy.

Charlotte Corday is here represented as a virgin assassin whose transparent pallor reflects candour and innocence, but also the irresponsibility of a sacred mission and gesture, choosing to commit murder in support of the Republic of which she should have been merely the faithful servant: Lamartine spoke of 'the heavenly beauty of love of country' which had spurred on 'this Joan of Arc in the service of freedom'. However, Mme Roland, painted by another woman, Mme Labille-Guiard, shows only conventional serenity, a fixed expression and gestures, quite incapable of capturing the passion, enthusiasm and fire devouring the woman who wrote: 'Wherever the wind may blow me, I carry with me the source of my joy.'

Charlotte Corday Having Just Assassinated Marat *(left)*, *anonymous painting, 18th Century. Paris, Carnavalet Museum*

A woman, called Madame Roland *(right)*, *Adélaïde Labille-Guiard. Quimper, Fine Arts Museum*

From the sky to the earth

—

Powers

Elisabeth Vigée-Lebrun painted Marie-Antoinette twenty times as a sovereign and mother in a state of majesty, in the fullness of the honours and privileges due to her rank. Beside her we see Madame Royale, and on her lap Louis-Charles, Duke of Normandy, born in 1785, the future Louis XVII. In 1794, in a white bonnet and a widow's veil, held prisoner in the Conciergerie, 'the widow Capet' has lost her queen's finery, but the woman condemned to the scaffold, whose gaze already seems to belong to another world, has kept the dignity and bearing required by her rank and the court society of which she was the model. Between these two representations should be placed all those which, from the mid-1770s, transformed 'the Austrian' into the woman who embodied all the scandals linked to royal power over the period during which its sacred aura disappeared.

At the Salon of 1787, when the painting by Vigée-Lebrun was exhibited in the Louvre, a visitor stuck a note on it reading 'Mrs Deficit'. In the pamphlets and lampoons which burgeoned after the Necklace Affair (1786), Marie-Antoinette was accused of ruining the kingdom through her extravagance. She remained the Plotter, the 'wicked queen', the 'stinking wild beast', the sovereign of a 'royal brothel', entirely given over to pleasure and to the 'bodily lusts' characteristic of her sex.

> – *The Comte d'Artois (brother of the king)*: 'Oh, what a bottom! How firm and springy!'
> – *The queen*: 'If my heart was as hard as that we'd be no good together.'
> – *The Comte d'Artois*: 'Shut up, you mad creature, or I'll give my brother another son this evening.'
> Anonymous pamphlet (1789)

Marie-Antoinette and Her Children *(left), Elisabeth Vigée-Lebrun, 1781. Château de Versailles*

Marie-Antoinette in the Conciergerie of Paris, *by Barthélemy Prieur, 1792(?). Versailles, Lambinet Museum*

From the sky to the earth

—

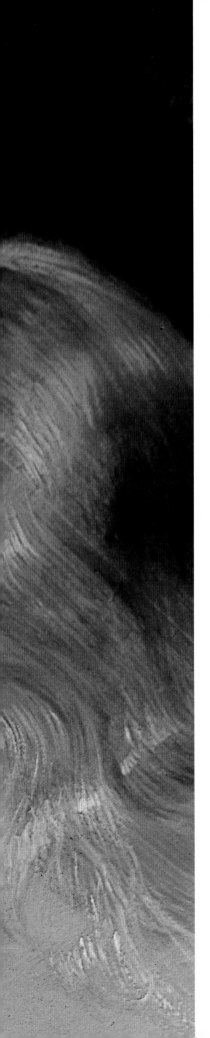

Beauty

The Toilet of Venus,
Peter-Paul Rubens, 1614.
Lichtenstein, Vaduz

For the Church, mirrors encourage the sin of vanity. They multiply one's image, that of the 'hateful I' denounced by Pascal in one of his *Pensées*. The interplay of looks and reflections, the use of colours to create the impression of desirable, sculptural, buxom flesh: the highlights are painted in thick, opaque layers, the shadows are thin and translucent. The optical effect suggests cold and pearliness through shadow, and the hot and the living through light emanating from the body. Everything here contributes to the exaltation of form and colour used to represent a woman heedless of the censures and prohibitions decreed by men of God.

But ultimately, what can be conveyed by the flood of words, of correlations, expert analyses, and interpretations? Are we sure that 'In the Beginning there was the Word'? Must images always stimulate words and writing? Must they be reduced to a commentary? Perhaps Van Gogh said it all when he saw *The Jewish Bride* in the Rijksmuseum in Amsterdam (p.125): 'I'd gladly give ten years of my life to stay here in front of this painting for a fortnight with some cheese and a loaf of bread.'

From the sky to the earth

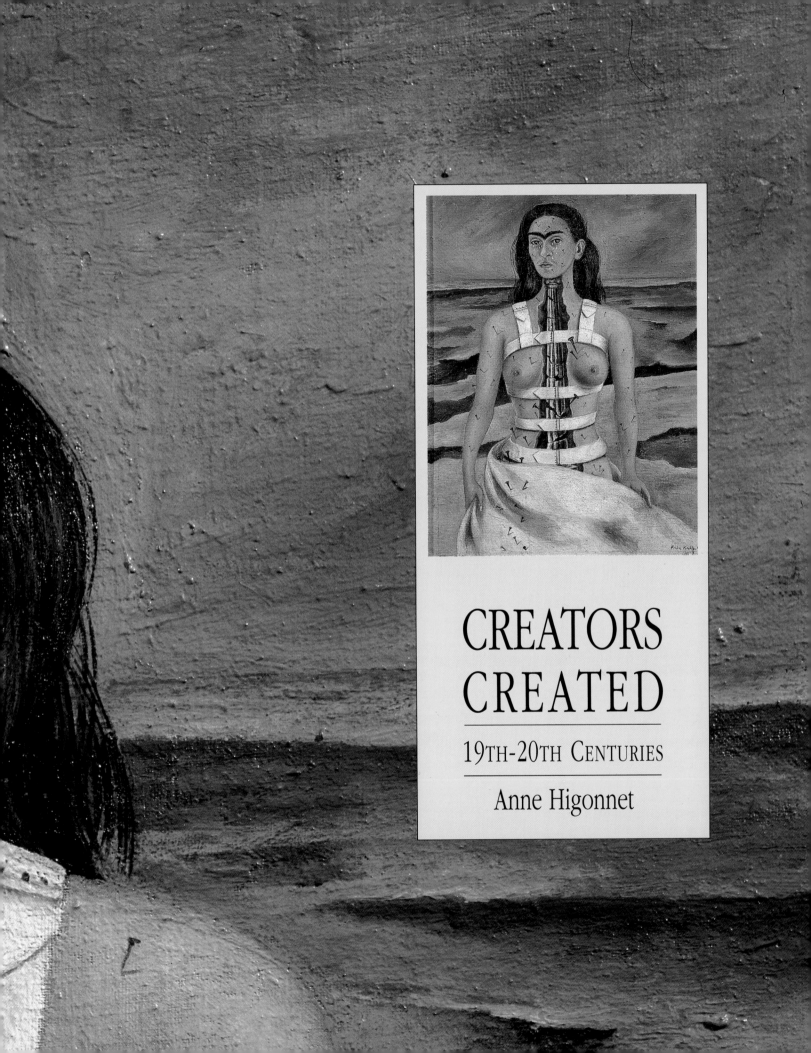

CREATORS
CREATED

19TH-20TH CENTURIES

Anne Higonnet

The image of woman in the 19th and 20th century seduces. Nowadays, we believe what we see with our own eyes. We live in the age of observation; science, philosophy, even literature guarantee the truth of what is seen. This visual proof is all the more persuasive since the means of creation now include the mechanical means of photographic reproduction. Nothing could be more automatic – it would seem. The effect of reality is even more convincing when the image represents a woman. We have invested the female image with beauty to such an extent that we can barely perceive it clearly. 'Beautiful', 'woman' and 'image' are almost interchangeable, they have been linked together so often. Men and women, we are all subject to the interconnected charms of the image and of the female beauty represented.

A certain mistrust of the modern image of woman will only add to the fun. Because, like any representation, a picture is a game, governed by cultural rules which have changed in the past and which will continue to change. The image of woman has a history – not as an illustration of the past, but a history of its own. The aim of this book is to sketch this history by means of a few examples. Fortunately, since it is a history, we do not have to make an arbitrary choice from among the innumerable beautiful women of our era. We must show the major visual themes of modern femininity. Let us begin with the dominant feature. In the 19th century, there was a consensus about the ideal woman: she was the middle-class woman in the home. We will look at paintings designed to show the harmonious balance of this symbol, but also at images of its extremes, of its fall and of the pleasure which can be derived therefrom. In order to understand the female ideal, it was necessary to see what the ideal was not. The image produces the difference, distinguishing women by age, class and race; in the same way, it shows us how to look at these distinctions, a point of view in the figurative sense as well as in the literal sense. Marginal aspects of women are brought to light by the differences in the images. More and more, the visual arts confront us with women and with women's experiences which were invisible in earlier society because the dominant modes of representation made them unimaginable. We desire to see. Therefore we see desire. Women look at each other with

Creators, created

—

new pleasure. These are the beginnings of what the 20th century will christen homosexuality. But, in a broader context, it is the beginning of an active gaze which can be enjoyed by women, a fertile gaze, of which artistic creation is the most developed form of expression. Twelve of the twenty-nine artists in this fourth section are women. The sexual models which ruled the arts and which allocated artistic creation to men and procreation to women are changing: all sexual models change, and the visual arts, so material, so tangible, so sensually close to sexuality, are paving the way. Abandoning religious or moral hindrances, painting, sculpture and photography vie with each other to adulate the female body. For the first time the nude is more likely to be a woman rather than a man. And never before have we seen so many male artists concentrating so intensely and so insistently on multiple images of a single woman. It seems that the gaze which the modern woman returns is not easily exhausted.

The Waltz, *sculpture by*
Camille Claudel, 1895.
Paris, Musée Rodin

Creators, created

Women at home

The radiant hearthside

Nineteenth-century painting has a single image to convey the expression 'home-maker'. And it is this image which is the most widespread during this era, throughout Europe, whether the artist is a man or a woman. The details of furniture, clothing and activity precisely convey the bourgeois nature of the scene; for example, the little desk, the pot plants, the simple, dark dress with the

white jabot and the peaceful work of sewing which we see in the picture by the Norwegian Harriet Backer.

The identity of the woman thus represented is understood by means of her visual relationship to the space and the objects in it. Who is the man unexpectedly arriving in the deliberately enigmatic picture by Ilya Repin? Contemporary Russians thought him to be a political exile pardoned after long years of suffering, now coming home.

Creators, created

—

142

The unexpected
visitor*(left), Ilya
Iefinovitch Repin,
1884. Moscow,
Tretiakov Gallery.*

Blue Interior *(right),*
Harriet Backer,
1883. Oslo,
National Gallery

Note that Repin chose the entry of a man into an interior inhabited above all by women to evoke a shock. The calm life of day-to-day domesticity thus reveals itself to be female; that which appears from outside is male, disturbing, perhaps political. Painters have taken this notion of the home as female territory to its limits. Whether oil or watercolour, the painting is flooded with light, which unites all the colours of the spectrum. Many artists, like Repin and Backer, emphasize the interiority of the picture's space by providing an external source of light. In the most subtle works, as again with our examples, these windows to the outside are themselves on the edge of the picture, and other allusions to exterior view – open doors, framed pictures and mirrors – reinforce the message of an enclosed, delimited scene.

Creators, created

House of suffering

In this essentially domestic object , we see paradoxically, the domestic ideal put to rout. The unknown artist has transformed the centre of the quilt into a parade of many different characters, animals and plants. The border is mysterious and somewhat disquieting. Near to idyllic trees, enormous serpents with forked tongues signal the arrival of something evil, whilst several adults show signs of anger: dilated nostrils and bulging eyes. A little girl, her arms outstretched, is pleading between a woman and a man, but nobody is listening to her. In the centre of the quilt, a female character apparently in distress, hands outstretched, wide eyed, is also placed between disagreeing couples; a turtle at her feet, two frogs at her side and a bird perched on her head symbolize some obscure preoccupation. Although there is no documentary proof, tradition has it that this central character is seen as the maker of the quilt, an unmarried girl who, around 1850 became pregnant and was commited to an asylum for the mentally ill in Catonsville, Maryland, were she died. The asylum is the building we can see in the quilt a little higher up and slightly to the left of the central character.[1] Made by someone who is marginalized in three ways – woman, unmarried mother, mentally ill – with materials which are themselves marginalized (scraps of cloth), this work seems to cry out to us, calling something almost inexpressible, something haunting.

Asylum Quilt (c.1850), maker unknown; cotton (226 x 200 cm). New York, Collection of America Hurrah Antiques

Creators, created

Maternity

Elena, third child of the Spanish painter Joaquin Sorolla, was born on 12 June 1895. Inspired by the event, Sorolla painted an image of maternity showing the joy of mother, father and painter. Like many *fin-de-siècle* painters, such as the American John Singer Sargent, the Swiss Anders Zorn and the Dane P.S. Krøyer, Sorolla paints realist subjects with a vigorous elegance, combining skilful workmanship with an almost abstract pictorial sensitivity. Here, almost all of the picture's surface is a flood of gold and blues, the broad, assured treatment of which seems spontaneous. In the midst of this free background, the baby's head, the mother's face and hands stand out thanks to their delicacy and their tonal warmth. By means of these contrasts, the painter conveys all the emotion of an instant. After the labour and the anguish of the delivery, there is rest and light. The mother proudly contemplates the small face of the new born child. They are two now, but still united in a world apart. The only witness to this intimacy, and almost sharing it since he is standing at the very edge of the bed, the painter declares himself the father. On the mother's finger shines a wedding ring, which Spanish women wear on the right hand. Sorolla exhibits his union with the mother with this shining detail which draws our attention to the tender and protective gesture of the image, to the paternal and artistic gesture which the image itself is. By its style and attitude, *The Mother* resumes the development of the theme of the Madonna. The subject of mother and child has lost none of its appeal, but its major modern versions are secular and individualized, they put the accent on the psychological and physical.

The Mother, *Joaquin Sorolla, 1895. Madrid, Sorolla Museum*

Women together
The invention of the little girl

Mother and Child *(left),*
Mary Cassatt, 1905.
Washington, National
Gallery of Art, Chester Dale
Collection

The Room *(right), Balthasar*
Klossowski, alias Balthus,
1952-1954. Private Collection

It was only towards the middle of the 19th century that the image of the little girl was invented. She is given a specific identity in various fields all at the same time: dress, painting, advertising and toys, in parallel with her literary and legal emergence.[2]

By far the majority of these images show the little girl as innocent, sweet. However, with psychoanalysis bringing the idea of individual identity closer to that of sexual identity and plunging its roots into childhood, we may wonder whether the current image of the little girl compensates, to some extent, for the anxiety aroused by exploration of female sexuality. Fairly rare, and therefore all the more influential, are images such as *Mother and Child* and *The Room*, which explore the identity of the little girl as an intrinsic phase of a woman's sexuality. For these two painters, the reflection on the status of the girl mutates into the presentation of the body as image. In the Cassatt, the mother encourages the child to look at herself in a mirror and this consciousness is directed to the spectator, who sees the reflected image of the little girl superimposed on the reflected image of the adult woman. In the Balthus, too, the body of the child, in a dark room, is offered up to a symbol of vision – the sunny window – by a double of herself, here a type of female gnome. We can only think of the famous 'stage of the mirror' of Lacan[3] and of the importance which he ascribes to the imago in the formation of the ego. But Lacan always speaks of a 'little man', and here we have little women. Note that the imagination of the male artist put female sexuality in direct contact with the natural light, whilst the female artist accentuates the artificial shifting of the eyes, the gaze of the girl and the link between her identity and her identification with the mother.

Classes

Even allowing for the eras which separate them, the women of Goya and of Hopper illustrate social differences. A *maya*, or prostitute, is leaning on her balcony, being shown off by an old procuress. The *maya* looks down on us from above, as if we were potential clients passing in the street. The glistening, amber tones of her complexion and dress draw our gaze to the space around her, a mysteriously dark place of illicit pleasures. For the moment she seems beautiful and fresh, but her companion foreshadows the degradation to come and warns us of the deceptive side of her appearance, to beware of the attraction which she inspires in us. Half hidden in the darkness of the image, ugly, degraded, greedy, Celestina represents the mercenary condition and the wretched future of prostitution. Judged from a moral point of view to be the lowest of the low, the prostitute is also the most frightening of women for the bourgeoisie, because her attractiveness can distort a man's judgement.

With Hopper we are still in the street, watching two women carry out their work. A pane of glass separates us from the waitress and cashier in a café. But, a century after Goya, we no longer have the same self-assurance. The social gulf between those looking at the picture and the subjects of the picture has narrowed noticeably. Moreover, in 1930 we are in the midst of an economic depression and, although the work shown is nothing wonderful, if we are in the street during the day it is probably because we have no work at all. However, the social distinctions persist. The waitress, the nearest to us in the fictitious space of the picture, is made subordinate in the visible hierarchy of the café by the way in which she is placed, leaning forward at the bottom of the composition. The seated cashier occupies the intermediate level, whilst the woman customer is the furthest away with her back to us. The title indicates another distinction, this time between men and women. 'Tables for Ladies' is a notice put in the window of an establishment where female customers are tolerated on condition that they occupy certain specific tables and do not go to the bar.

Celestina and her girl (left),
Francisco Goya, 1808-1812.
Madrid, Private Collection

Creators, created

—

Tables for Ladies (right), Edward Hopper,
1930. New York, The Metropolitan
Museum of Art, George A. Hearn Fund, 1931

Creators, created

Race

The orientalist fantasy implies femininity. Ingres presents three slaves: an odalisque, a servant girl and a eunuch. They occupy the harem, a place which is so evocative for a European audience. All the trappings of the image are there: dense greenery, cushions, exotic musical instrument, hookah, fan, jewels, silks. The wealth of textures, geometric designs, contrasting colours, and voluptuous folds creates a world of surfaces, a decor which conveys the western idea of a passive Orient, indolent and sensual. The man is almost not a man, the women are only there to please us. Feminized, the Orient becomes desirable.

The image establishes a visual correlative to the racial difference, hierarchical power and sexual desire. The black eunuch, in the background, serves both women. Obeying European rules of perspective, there then follows the swarthy musician – beautiful but withdrawn. She serves the object presented to of our gaze – the white woman stretched out before us across the whole picture. Her sharp profile, the roundness of her form, the transparent wrap which clings to her body, her skin as pure as marble – it all conveys the artistic ideal of Graeco-Roman sculpture. These neo-classical references, introduced into the image of the oriental harem, only serve to strengthen the fantastical quality of the picture. Evocations of age, class or race assume their full strength when art links them together.

Interior of a harem with an odalisque *Jean-Dominique Ingres, 1842.*
Baltimore, Walters Gallery

Mutual desires

Homosexuality is a term introduced by psychoanalysis. But, even if lesbianism was a rarity before the 20th century, one can observe mutual attraction between women. Excluded from male professions and society, middle-class women were forced into a life which could be described as homosocial. The transports of affection which marked their relationships seemed perfectly acceptable because they were covered by the code of sentimentality. Meanwhile, in the particular field of the visual, access to the image-related professions enabled them to produce something which conveyed and magnified the desire into an image. The new technology of photography, in particular, did not require any professional training, which was at that time the preserve of men. Thus, throughout the 19th century, one discovers images like those of the Englishwoman, Lady Hawarden, where the two sisters' loving gesture becomes the physical equivalent of the look which one of the sisters exchanges with the photographer, who is her mother.

When, in the next century, a woman tries to express her desire for other women, she will use means which are more sexual but less feminine. Tamara de Lempicka shows the *Duchesse de la Salle* in riding clothes, a recognized sign of a lesbian. Her open-necked shirt, her casually self-confident pose and the way she is showing her thigh reinforce the image of dominating sexuality. But the very masculinity of her behaviour keeps this sexuality under the control of men. The aspects of the portrait which promise emancipation from the dominant models of representation are those which it shares with Hawarden's photograph – the exchange of direct glances between women, which structures our perception of the image, and the urban location of this exchange, sign of the modern condition.

Two sisters on a balcony
*(left), photograph by Lady
Hawarden, circa 1865.
London, Victoria and Albert
Museum*

The Duchesse de la Salle
*(right), Tamara de Lempicka,
1925. Hamburg, Private
Collection, courtesy of Barry
Friedman Ltd. New York*

Who am I?
Transformations

How to express an ego that does not exist? Woman's experience rejects the rules of art; her work distorts the conventions of femininity. For Marcello and for Bernhardt, the answer, like the question, lies in transformation – of subjects, of forms and of genders. Marcello (pseudonym of Adèle d'Affry, Duchess of Colonna) exhibited her *Pythia* at the Paris Salon of 1870. Her challenge to the bastion of official art was even more striking because her sculpture of the sibyl, the oracle of Delphi, for Garnier's Opéra was a prestigious public commission. At the time, hardly any women would have dared to practise publicly an art form considered to be so masculine. For what she considered her masterpiece, Marcello chose the theme of the woman possessed by a force which she cannot control; woman is only the voice of divine inspiration. Marcello literally put herself into her work: the arms, shoulders and feet of the original plaster cast were moulded on herself.

Primarily an actress, Sarah Bernhardt was also a sculptress. In 1879 she was rehearsing the role of a heroine who wears a poison ring shaped like a sphinx. In her *Fantastic Inkwell* she gave her own face to a sphinx with the wings of a griffon; she then decorated this metamorphosed self-portrait with a goblin and added the masks of comedy and tragedy. A little ornament and a man-killer at the same time, the *Fantastic Inkwell* takes pleasure in contradictions. The head of the actress, destined to play roles written by others, has become an object in the service of writing, source of ink and holder of pen. Or perhaps the writer's pen is merely an ornament for the divine and protean Sarah?

Creators, created

Fantastic Inkwell
*front and profile (left),
self portrait as sphinx,
bronze by Sarah
Bernhardt, 1880. Boston,
Museum of Fine Arts*

Pythia *(detail,
right), bronze by
Marcello, 1870.
Paris, Palais Garnier*

Self-portrait *(left), Lynda Benglis, advertisement published in* Artforum *in November 1974*

Untitled, *1977,* Arbol de la vida *series (centre), work* 'of earth and body with fabric', *executed in Oaxaca, Mexico by Ana Mendieta. Courtesy of the Estate of Ana Mendieta and Lelong Gallery, New York*

The body in question

In November 1974, the fashionable art magazine *Artforum* published an article on the minimalist work of Benglis. The artist wanted the photograph opposite included in the article; when the editor refused, she and her gallery transformed the image into an advertisement which appeared in the same number. Some critics, *Artforum* writers included, protested against this scheme. Evidently Benglis' gesture had shown just how easy it is to cross the border between art criticism and paid advertising. More serious still, she had made her gesture of economic power via a powerful image of her superb body, gleaming like her sculptures and ironically displaying the forbidden phallus. Suddenly the New York avant-garde, who considered themselves the defenders of abstraction and motivated by pure intellectual conviction, were assailed by the social stench of an image which was accused of vulgarity and a feminism which rejected pretensions to sexual neutrality.

During the same period, Mendieta was looking for almost opposite ways of empowering the female body. Instead of amplifying it in a hybrid form, she merged it into nature. By leaving her print or her silhouette on water, earth, fire, stone and here sand, she captured fleeting traces of them with photography. Some of her images are recognizably female, but for Mendieta woman has an archaic power which predates society.

X-Ray *(right)*
sculpture by Lynda Benglis,
in aluminium and plaster
(140 x 50 x 35 cm),
1973 - 1974.
New York, Paula Cooper
Gallery

Creators, created

Women of love
Creation

He can do anything, where she is concerned.
The Greek myth of Pygmalion retains its place in the
imagination of the modern artist. Gérôme gives us a
grandiose archaeological version. The sculptor sees his
prayer to the gods answered: the marble of the ideal
woman comes to life under his passionate kiss. Magritte
repeats the theme a century later in a more austere
manner, substituting the painter for the sculptor. The
style of precise realism which both artists adopt lends
itself to the illusion. For both of them, the subject
expresses the potential of the magic power which the
artist dreams of and also the link between this dream
and male sexual desire. The ultimate work would be of
a woman whose perfection is entirely the product of a
man's imagination. For men and for women, the free
gift of creation still contains something of the
miraculous.

*Attempting
the Impossible (right),
René Magritte, 1928.
Private collection*

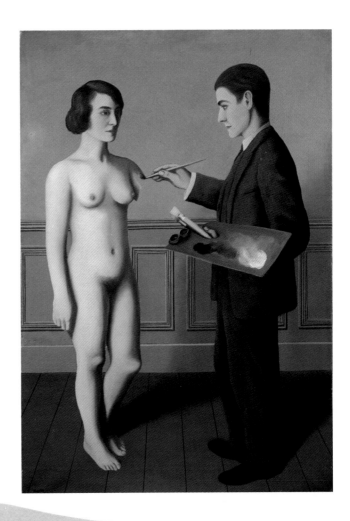

*Pygmalion and Galatea (left),
Jean-Léon Gérôme, 1890.
New York, The Metropolitan
Museum of Art*

Creators, created

—

Inspiration

In 1848 a group of young English people dedicated themselves to art. They named themselves the Pre-Raphaelite Brotherhood, to indicate their allegiance to what they considered a level of perfection which had disappeared with the Renaissance. Ideal female beauty was an essential element in this perfection. In practice, the Pre-Raphaelites showed themselves to be almost obsessed by a small group of real women whom they painted in multiple guises, and whose particular traits have become the signature of the whole movement.

Millais' work was one of the greatest successes of the era. This painting portrays the triumphant love of a Scotswoman in the 18th century. Her husband had been imprisoned for having taken part in the Jacobite rising. Although of very humble background, she has obtained a release warrant which she is holding out to the guard. In the centre of the picture, the dog, symbol of loyalty, draws our attention to the couple's entwined hands. The model who posed for the virtuous Scotswoman was Effie Ruskin, wife of John Ruskin, the influential critic. Shortly afterwards, she married Millais.

For Proserpine, Rossetti also chose a model he was in love with: Jane Morris, the wife of another Pre-Raphaelite, William Morris. For having tasted the pomegranate, Proserpine was sentenced to spend several months of the year with the king of the dead. The split fruit in the centre of Rossetti's picture assumes all the latent sensuality of his idol, mythological symbol of female sexuality.

Creators, created

The Order of Release
(left), John E. Millais,
1852. London, Tate
Gallery

Proserpine *(right),*
Dante Gabriel Rossetti,
1874. London, Tate
Gallery

Victims of desire

These women are branded by lust. Munch crudely worked the wood in his plank, using the force of the cut to form the hatching for the shadows and the spermatic shapes on the border. The ink of the printing press leaves a black smear on the arm of Meret Oppenheim, the surrealist Swiss artist who was Man Ray's model. The techniques involved in the images, engraving tools in the 19th century, mechanical methods for photography in the 20th century, convey the fantasy of possession. The ambiguity launches the imagination without directing it. A madonna with a sickly foetus... The silently threatening wheel with its handle which thrusts sex towards us... After these images, look again at the self-representations of Benglis and Mendieta.

Madonna *(left),*
Edvard Munch, 1895.
Oslo, Munch Museum

Érotique violée (right),
photograph by Man Ray,
1933. Paris, Private
Collection

Creators, created

Obsession

Salvador Dali is one of many modern artists for whom a woman has inspired many portraits, even a major part of his work. In this one volume we have the Pre-Raphaelite paintings of Effie Ruskin and Jane Morris, the photograph of Meret Oppenheim by Man Ray and of Lella by Boubat, all bearing witness to the reality of this phenomenon; and the self-portrait of Frida Kahlo reminds us that a woman artist could well become obsessed with her own person. Evidently these women, often artists themselves, were no longer the discreet muses of earlier times, Galatea figures, they were motivated by their own creative will. Rembrandt could paint a series of moving portraits of his wife Saskia without her seeming responsible for them; Dali has always attributed his career to Gala. The moral support is invisible, but the face and body of Gala haunt her husband's work across the decades.

If Dali worked like so many others by identifying the woman with the image, he did it knowingly, combining the duality of Gala with his references to the history of art. Each new Gala passes through the process of repeating the established images. Following the example of the anatomical engravings of the 18th century, in 1945 Dali takes the framework for a double of Gala from architecture (comparable to *The Broken Column* by Kahlo); the two 1935 Galas, seated facing each other, already reflect the Millet hanging behind them; in 1952, in the *The Madonna of Port Lligart*, Gala becomes the Madonna. The being which she carries within her becomes divine itself. Dali's surrealism shows us a representation of a woman made up of scattered elements drawn from our visual imagination.

My wife, nude, contemplating her own flesh becoming stairs, three vertebrae of a column sky and architecture *(left)*, *Salvador Dali, 1945.* *Private Collection*

Portrait of Gala, *Salvador Dali, 1935.* *New York, Museum of Modern Art*

Mourning

Love which survives death is beautiful. The image of the woman in mourning for her lost husband is a constant source of emotion.

In the 19th century, death is a personal drama, as seen in the painting by Tissot, lived according to the rules of the middle-class family. The widow is seen in a retreat in the park with a young girl and an old woman at her side. Her situation takes its place in the cycle of a woman's life. The moment is set, unique, with a profusion of realistic details. The painting offers us a window to intimacy.

A century later, Warhol makes the widow the public figure of a political drama. In the centre of the picture, the smiling face of Jacqueline Bouvier Kennedy, wife of the President of the USA, John Fitzgerald Kennedy, on 22 November 1963 in Dallas In the top right-hand corner, in the centre and in the bottom left, it is still Jacqueline with her husband barely recognizable. They are in the car in which John Kennedy will be assassinated in a few moments. In the top left-hand corner, and in the bottom right, Jacqueline at three different points during the funeral ceremony. By means of chronological succession, repetition and the simplification of images which have become icons, known throughout the world from television and the press, Warhol is playing on the way the media highjacks tragedy and saturates our visual imagination. In the 19th as in the 20th century, the drama of death within conjugal love is part of a social and political scene.

The Widow *(left),*
James Tissot, 1868.
London, Roy Miles Gallery

Nine Jackies *(right),*
silk-screen process on
canvas,
Andy Warhol, 1964.
Paris, Galerie Sonnaben

Creators, created

Powers

Kruger's work could well serve as a caption to that of Delacroix: 'Your body is a battleground'. Sardanapalus, absolute ruler of Assyria, sees his enemies about to invade his palace. He orders the destruction of his treasures and the death of his horses and slaves. Everything must perish with him, for him. Unmoved, reclining, enthroned on his couch, his power can be seen in the foreground, in the violence inflicted on the exposed body of a woman. In order to work counter to the attitudes which we inherit from the history of art, Kruger uses images of the past, superimposing her verbal invocations. Of course, Delacroix's painting implicitly addresses a viewer who is designated by the space of the picture as the reflection of Sardanapalus himself. However, Kruger explicitly addresses the audience: 'your body'. And often, as here, she dwells, quite literally, on the negative side of the images found. The result is modern, but the stakes shown are ancient.

Death of Sardanapale,
Eugène Delacroix, 1827.
Paris, Louvre

Untitled *(top right), photo*
on silk and vinyl screen,
Barbara Kruger, 1989. New
York, Mary Boone Gallery

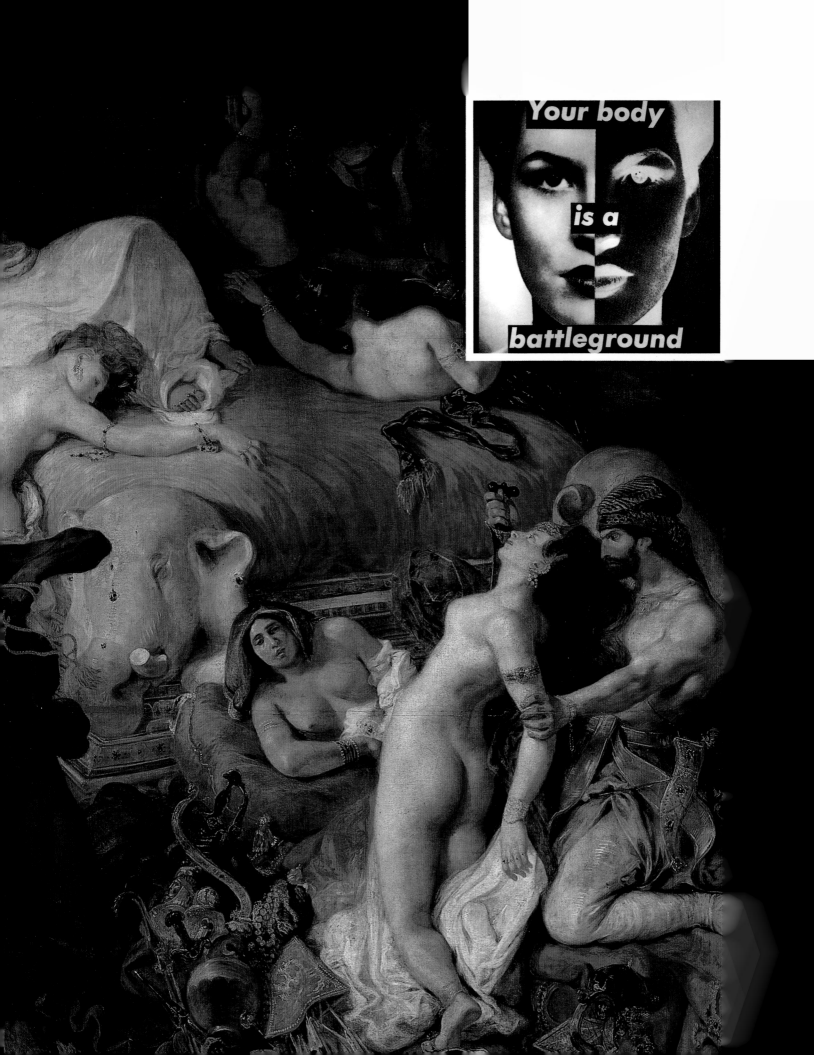

Beauty

Lella, *photograph
by Edouard Boubat,
1945-1950*

Beauty is proverbially in the eye of the beholder. No one image could satisfy all the ideals which have proliferated since the 18th century and modern individualism would reject any topology of beauty. Nevertheless, this photograph by Edouard Boubat could sum up the difference between the new and the old criteria of female beauty. Before our era, this woman would certainly not have been considered beautiful. None of the signs so essential to the old standards of beauty - whether it be luxury, seductiveness, male admiration, deification or a family role – are present here. What can we know of this woman, who is not placed in any defined situation? To what social milieu, to what class does she belong? Is she single, married, widowed, a mother?

The photographer has chosen to portray her from below, so that her profile is outlined heroically against the sky, hair blowing in the wind. She has sometimes been christened 'Solitude' or 'Freedom', but she hardly resembles the traditional allegories from history, such as the famous 'Liberty' of Delacroix. Alone and free, yes, Boubat's version of woman is all of this – in the sense of a thoroughly contemporary independence and autonomy.

Women and their Images
or a Woman's Gaze

MICHELLE PERROT

In this book an attempt has been made to answer the question: 'What are the main – or marginal – ways in which men (because it is almost exclusively men) represent women and how should these representations be interpreted?' The criterion of representation has taken precedence over the criterion of beauty, even if – it is hoped – it did not replace it. In fact beauty has been a dominant feature in this book. This cross-fertilization of representation and beauty has not simplified our task.

So what is beauty? 'A promise of happiness', said Stendhal, referring to the area of sexual desire. The sense of well-being or pain which we experience when contemplating an object, a landscape, a harmoniously formed creature, this harmony itself being perhaps nothing more than conformity to the standards of an era. Because a gaze is just as tyrannical as it is subservient. To free someone from this, 'One is implored to close one's eyes', said Freud. And Levinas said, 'The best way to deal with other people is to not even look at the colour of their eyes.' Because attractiveness is violent, too.

At the very heart of this passion, we find ... women. In the duality which since the creation of the world has opposed male to female, beauty is associated with women as strength is associated with men. Woman incorporates Beauty; Woman is Beauty incarnate. She adorns the sky and the earth, in the same way as she must adorn the town and the home. The spent warrior, the exhausted hunter, the weary traveller, the overworked manager; to all of them she offers the smooth softness of her smiling face (laughter deforms; it belongs to men, or to the devil), or the tender dew of her tears. She offers the haven of her body, a body of secret places. The unveiling of these secret places, strictly codified by current propriety, is a source of pleasure, crude or refined according to the *ars erotica* which distinguishes civilizations; and the way in which that changes is in itself an indication of the relationships between men and women.

Images of women express, or suggest, the dreams, hopes and fears of men. God created Woman? The artist, the demiurge, is still re-creating her. Within this endless panorama, made up of repetitions, reminiscences, modulated variations and violent breaks, the historian, a dazzled spectator, tries to identify what is permanent and those changes where structures of a coded language and the expression of new sensitivities mix in an almost inextricable manner. But can we get to the other side of the mirror? How have women themselves viewed and experienced their portrayal? What did they think? To what extent have they tried to conform to or to hide from those models, whether suggested to them or forced on them? Have the unattainable ideals of body and of dress caused them to suffer? How have they tried to bend them, to control the limitations, to use them, to enjoy them, or to subvert them? In short, how did they view them? We have very little information on this essential dimension of the story, simply because very little research has been done. In general, very few questions have been asked about the social usages of the image and even fewer, probably none at all, about its sexual usages.[1]

Until such an investigation is undertaken we can only seize on a few traces of the interest which women show in how they are represented, in either mundane or more elevated contexts: what is perhaps the self-portrait of a medieval scribe in the illuminated capital letter of a psalter; the protestations of Florentine ladies against the laws which forced them into dark, unadorned dresses; elsewhere, the petition from French women complaining to the king about the constraints of appearance: 'If nature has not granted them beauty, women get married without dowry to poor tradesmen and vegetate miserably in the depths of the provinces, bearing children they are unable to raise. If, on the other hand, they are born beautiful, they fall prey to the first seducer.'[2] Only recently, Sandrine Bonnaire, confronted like other young actresses with the misogyny of producers and, like them, determined assert her right to recognition as a talented individual, rebelled: 'It does not matter if people find me ugly. After all, it is more important to be a person than an image.'[3]

For women, image is first and foremost tyranny. It confronts them with an ideal, whether physical or related to dress. It tells them what is good and what is beautiful: how to behave, how to dress, according to age, class, social or marital status, according to place and to time. It is on women that the critical gaze of family, neighbours and the general public rests. Of course, the power of images changes with time according to the importance of the body and of beauty in the sexual market place or social scene, and in accordance with the amount of visual promotion by the advertising media. Presumably images were of less significance when mirrors were a rarity and long mirrors unknown – George Sand saw herself full-length for the first time at the age of four, in 1808, in a mirror in a royal palace in Spain - at a time when the poorest in society saw no images at all of themselves other than in the opacity of a window pane or on the surface of an expanse of still water. Being associated with washing-places and village fountains, did women have an awareness of their own looks? So what would their perception of a face have been like? The world of pictured images would have been a universe in its own right, separate, and truly imaginary; an other-world, mysterious and distant, quite separate from everyday life. Beauty is inaccessible, useless, even threatening, as we hear so often in country proverbs: 'Fluffy clouds and a painted face do not last long'; 'A beautiful wife makes for a troubled marriage'; 'Handsome is as handsome does'.

The increase in the number of all kinds of images, which exploded in the 19th century – 'Glorifying the cult of the image', according to Baudelaire – had contradictory effects, increasing at one and the same time the meaningfulness of the models and that of the rules and the power of the identity games. Whilst painting was leaving the elevated areas of religion and the historical epic to become cosy and familiar, and whilst a taste for portraits was developing, both satisfied and stimulated by photography, fashion and its arbitrary demands, spread by women's magazines, now entered the lives of a growing number of women, enslaved, (un)happily to a greater or lesser extent, by the commandments of imitation and distinctiveness. 'A woman's clothing must have a gender. A woman must be a woman from the top of her head to the tips of her toes',[4] wrote Sébastien Mercier at the time of the Enlightenment. This sculpting of appearance even extends to the body itself, which is divided into sections and shaped according to a set of rules. Physiognomy scrutinizes faces, palmistry examines hands, detailed anthropometry sets the ideal measurements, an instrument of torture for those who would aspire to the title of 'Beauty Queen', the symbolic triumph of the accepted standard. The ideal of slimness, cause of anorexia (a form of female depression), is the most extreme sign of the trap set by images. From this trap stems the increase in anxiety which women, henceforth assigned to beauty, feed by worrying about their appearance. Those unable or unwilling to conform are ridiculed. 'These Republican women wearing their rosettes are fearfully ugly', said a revolutionary. And of course, political spokeswomen, feminists, schoolteachers, bluestockings, are invariably repulsive. Fear of being ugly, fear of growing old, become women's fears.

However, the image can also be a source of pleasure: there is pleasure in being portrayed, celebrated, embellished, the Virgin in the cathedral porch, the lady on the frescos of a palace or stitched into a tapestry, a heroine, or an ordinary woman portrayed in the cornice of a museum; Baudelaire wrote that these were the only proper places for a woman. Women were undoubtedly not insensitive to the beauty of their own sex, no more so than to the games of flirtation and the charms of seduction, a subtle form of power, nowadays extended to everyone in society, to the point where some sociologists speak of the 'feminization' of society (cf. Baudrillard, Maffesoli). Young girls' education, in the shadows, amongst the whispers of the sewing-room and in the perfumed salons, meant that the most modest of women were initiated very early on into a whole range of olfactory and tactile sensations; in particular they became familiar with a universe of textiles, shimmering and colourful - linen and other fabrics, ribbons, trimmings, cottons and printed chintzes which young country girls in the 18th century dreamed of - the longing for these or the greedy possession of them was an expression of female sensuality. 'My heart fluttered, thinking how pretty I would look: my hand trembled with every pin I attached',[5] said Marianne de Marivaux, subtle interpreter of the new games of love. Awareness of one's self-image brings with it the desire to manage the image, even to manufacture it. The Florentines of the quattrocento rebelled against the austere ordinances which forbade their luxurious display - the classic theme of the merchants and the moralists. They increased the number of already 'proliferate tricks' to evade the regulations, sent in petitions and, via their spokesperson, Nicolosa Sanuti, raised a solemn protest: 'We shall do our utmost to stop our ornaments and our finery being snatched from us, because they are the insignia of our virtues'.[6] The deliberate fullness of the farthingale allowed them to hide the fruit of their illicit loves. 'By means of their clothing, women participated visibly in the act of self-creation, which according to Burckhardt was a decisive trait of Renaissance culture',[7] wrote Diane Hughes, the historian. Christine de Pizan also emphasized the right to be beautiful for one's own sake. She painted herself in miniatures, like Clara Peters, the 18th-century still-life painter who repeated her face seven times on the sides of a goblet:[8] an expression of the female claim of the right to a portrait, which, although always present, increased during the 19th century.

In order to change images, it is necessary to possess them. The story of women's conquest of the image is less well known than their conquest of literature, and more painful, to judge from the sad story of

Camille Claudel. That book remains to be written: fragments of it can be found here.[9] In painting, photography (considered for a long time to be a secondary form of art, and therefore more open), the cinema especially, advertising and even cartoons (the wonderful talent of Claire Bretécher), women's progress has been substantial but still marginal, so strong is institutionalized inertia and the opposition they face. And they have made very few changes to the way they are represented or to the visual universe in general, which is still largely the work of men. The road has been opened, but it will be a long one and it will be a long time before women gain access to the world of Creation, this divine area, so long forbidden to them ... and when by incorporating these strangled voices, these different perceptions and experiences, even this strangeness, art will become truly universal, encompassing all the Beauty of the world.

Notes

Myths and mysteries
1.   Strabon, VII, 2, 3.
2.   Psalms, 21.

Society depicted
1.   Identification of the scene is thanks to Eliana Carrara, *Schifanoia* (1992).

From the sky to the earth
1.   Quoted by Jacques Thuillier, *Fragonard*, Paris, Skira, 1967, p. 113

Creators, created
1.   This information comes from Sandi Fox, *Wrapped in Glory : Figurative Quilts and Bedcovers 1700-1900*, Los Angeles and New York, Los Angeles County Museum and Thames & Hudson, 1990, pp. 76-78.
2.   Nicole Savy, *Les Petites Filles modernes*, Dossiers du Musée d'Orsay, Paris, Éditions de la Réunion des Musées nationaux, 1989
3.   Jacques Lacan, Écrits, Paris, Éditions du Seuil, 1966, pp. 89-97

Women and Their Images
or a Woman's Gaze
1.   For a recent attempt - more political and social than sexual - see Stéphane Michaud, Jean-Yves Mollier and (edited by) Nicole Savy, *Usages de l'image au XIXe siècle*, preface by Maurice Agulhon, Paris, Créaphis, 1992. For contemporary thoughts on Beauty, cf. Nicole Czechowski and Véronique Nahoum-Grappe, 'Fatale Beauté', *Autrement (91)*, June 1987; Olivier Burgelin and (edited by) Philippe Perrot, 'Parure, Pudeur, Etiquette', *Communications (46)*, 1987.
2.   Quoted by Véronique Nahoum-Grappe, 'La Belle femme', *Histoire des femmes en Occident*, Book III, 6th-8th centuries, edited by Arlette Farge and Natalie Zemon Davis, p. 95.
3.   *Marie-France*, 'Stars sans fard, La nouvelle génération de comédiennes du cinéma français', study by Thérèse Fournier, p. 40.
4.   Quoted by Françoise Borin, 'Arrêt sur image', *Histoire des femmes en Occident*, Book III, 6th-8th centuries, p. 239.
5.   Marivaux, *La Vie de Marianne*, Paris, Flammarion, 1978, p. 82. Quoted by Sylvia Ostrowetsky, unpublished text 'La Laideur'.
6.   Quoted by Diane Hughes, 'Les Modes', *Histoire des femmes en Occident*, Book II, The Middle Ages, edited by Christiane Klapisch-Zuber, p. 165.
7.   Ibid, p. 167
8.   *Histoire des femmes en Occident*, Book III, 6th-8th centuries, Fig. 36.
9.   And in various volumes of *Histoire des femmes en Occident*, especially Book IV, The 19th century, Anne Higonnet, 'Femmes et Images. Apparences, loisirs, subsistance'. Research underway on women and painting in the 19th century, by Denise Noël; on 'Les femmes photographes en France au XIXe siècle', cf. dissertation by Françoise Condé, Paris VII, 1992.

The authors

In order of appearance in the book

Georges Duby

Of the Académie Française and Member of the Institute, Professor of History of Medieval Societies at the Collège de France since 1970; he has also been a lecturer in the history of the Middle Ages at the faculty of arts in Aix-en-Provence since 1953.

His numerous works include (published in Paris): *l'An Mil*, 1967; *Guerriers et paysans, essai sur la première croissance économique de l'Europe*, 1973; *les Trois Ordres ou l'imaginaire du féodalisme*, 1978; *le Chevalier, la femme et le prêtre*, 1981 ; *Guillaume le Maréchal ou le meilleur chevalier du monde*, 1984 . He also co-edited *l'Histoire de la France rurale*, 1975; *l'Histoire de la France urbaine*, 1980; *l'Histoire de la vie privée*, 1985. He is co-editor of *Histoire des femmes en Occident*, 5 vols., Paris, 1991-1992, with Michelle Perrot.

Chiara Frugoni

Professor of Medieval History at the University of Rome II, where she lectures on the psychologies of the Middle Ages. She is researching iconography of the 9th to 14th centuries. She has published *Una lontana città, sentimenti ed immagini nel Medioevo*, 1983; *Francesco: Un'altra storia*, 1988. She is the co-author of *Histoire des femmes en Occident*, Book II, *Moyen Age*, Paris, 1991, edited by Christiane Klapisch-Zuber, for which she wrote the commentary on iconography: Chapter 11, 'La femme imaginée'.

Michel Rouche

Lecturer at the University of Paris I-Sorbonne, he is a specialist of the Late Roman Empire and the High Middle Ages. His thesis was on 'Aquitaine, from the Visigoths to the Arabs (418-781)'. He is the author of *Empires universels*, Paris, 1969; *l'Europe au Moyen Age*, Paris, 1969; *Des barbares à la Renaissance*, Paris, 1991. He has also worked on book 1 of *Moyen Age*, 3 vols., 1981-1982, edited by Robert Fossier and on *Malheurs des temps*, Paris, 1986, edited by J. Delumeau.

Joël Cornette

Senior lecturer at the University of Paris I-Sorbonne since 1989, he has first and foremost published work on the power of the royal family and the state in the 17th century: 'Fiction et réalité de l'Etat baroque (1610 - 1652)' in *Etat baroque, regards sur la pensée politique de la France du premier XVIIe siècle*, Paris, 1985; *l'Etat classique*, Paris, 1992, in collaboration with Henry Méchoulan; *le Roi de guerre, essai sur le pouvoir royal et ses représentations*, Paris, 1992.

The authors

(continued)

Anne Higonnet

Assistant Professor at Wellesley College, Department of Art, where she teaches the history of visual culture in the 19th and 20th centuries. Her biography of the impressionist painter Berthe Morisot was published in France in 1990, and her study of images of women was published in the USA in 1992. She is co-author of *Histoire des femmes en Occident*, in Book IV, *XIXe siècle*, edited by Geneviève Fraisse and Michelle Perrot, Paris, 1991 (Chaps. 11 and 12 'Femmes et images') and in Book V, *XXe siècle*, edited by Françoise Thébaud, Paris, 1992 (Chap. 12 'Femmes, images et représentations').

Michelle Perrot

Lecturer in Contemporary History at the University of Paris VII-Jussieu. Following initial research on the world of the working class in the 19th century (*les Ouvriers en grève*, Paris, 1974), she turned her attention to the study of delinquency and penal systems: *l'Impossible Prison*, 1980; *Ecrits pénitentiaires d'Alexis de Tocqueville*, Book IV, 2 vols. of *Oeuvres complètes*, Paris, 1984, published by M.P.; then to *l'Histoire de la vie privée* (Book IV – 19th century – from the series edited by Ph. Ariès and G. Duby, Paris, 1987), and in particular to the history of women: *Lettres des filles de Karl Marx*, Paris, 1979; *Journal intime de Caroline B.* (with Georges Ribeill), Paris, 1985; *Une histoire des femmes est-elle possible?*, Marseille, 1984. She co-edited *l'Histoire des femmes en Occident*, 5 vols., Paris 1991-1992, with Georges Duby.

Photographic References

Artephot, Babey: 58, 59d. Bridgeman : 136, 142, 143, 163. Brumaire : 109. Fabbri: 88. Held: 51, 124m, 124d, 125, 126, 153, 169. Kumasegawa : 164. Martin : 166, 167. Nimatallah : 68-69, 93, 106d, 115, 118, 119, 124g. Oronoz: 59g, 150. Takase : 83. Bibliothèque d'Art et d'Archéologie : 128. Bibliothèque municipale de Poitiers : 56. Bibliothèque nationale : 65, 97, 129. Bildarchiv Preussischer Kulturbesitz : 123, 127. Bridgeman Art Gallery : 168. British Museum : 52, 53. Bulloz : 16, 19, 21, 26, 29. Charmet : 130. Claire Bretécher : 17.
Collection of America Hurrah Antiques, N.Y.C.: 144, 145. Courtesy The Estate of Ana Mendietta and Galerie Lelong, N.Y. : 158-159.
Dagli Orti 9, 15, 25, 34-35, 37, 38d, 39g, 40, 41, 42, 44, 45, 46, 47, 48, 50, 57, 64, 66, 67, 72-73, 74, 75, 76, 77, 78, 79, 80, 82, 84, 86, 87, 89, 91, 94, 99, 100, 101, 102-103, 107, 110, 111, 112, 116, 117, 132, 134, 135, 138-139, 170-171. Explorer, Moatti : 157. Giraudon : 12, 31, 39d, 90, 95, 98, 133. Lauros : 70, 149. Photothèque René Magritte : 161. Labat : 38g, 54. Magnum, Lessing : 43, 61, 81, 85, 92, 96, 106g, 113. Mary Boone Gallery, New York : 171. Metropolitan Museum of Art : 160. Musée Rodin : 33. Denis Bernard/Christian Bonnard :141. Museo Sorolla, Aranda : 147. Museum of Fine Arts, Boston, The Photographic Services Department, MFA : 156. Museum of Modern Art: 151. National Gallery of Arts, Photographic Service :148. Paula Cooper Gallery, N.Y.C.:159d; Gordon :158g. Private Collection, Hamburg-Courtesy of Barry Friedman Ltd., New York: 155. Rijksmuseum : 122. R.M.N.: 105, 120, 121 . Jean : 62, 63. Roger-Viollet : 10. Scala : 55,108. Staatliche Kunsthalle, Karlsruhe : 131. Tate Gallery, J.Webb : 162. TMR/ADAGP, Paris, 1992, Collection L.Treillard : 165. Top, Boubat : 172. Victoria and Albert Museum, Picture Library : 155.

ADAGP : Lynda Benglis © 1992 : 158, 159 ; Salvador Dali © 1992 : 166, 167 ; René Magritte © 1992 : 161 ; © Man Ray Trust, Paris, 1992 : 165 ; Joachim Sorolla © 1992 : 147 ; Andy Warhol, © 1992 : 169.

SPADEM : Balthus, Balthazar Klossowski de Rola dit, © 1992 : 149 ; Camille Claudel © 1992 : 141; Tamara de Lempicka © 1992 : 155 ; Aristide Maillol © 1992 : 26 ; Pablo Picasso © 1992 : 31.

Barbara Kruger: 'Untitled' (Your body is a battleground), 112" by 112" photographic silkscreen / vinyl, 1989. Courtesy : Mary Boone Gallery, New York : p.171

Tamara de Lempicka, Polish 1898-1980 : Duchesse de La Salle, oil on canvas, 1925, signed at top right : T. de Lempicka, size : 63$^{1}/_{2}$" by 37 $^{3}/_{4}$", Private Collection, Hambourg, Courtesy of Barry Friedman Ltd., New York : 155.

Ana Mendietta, Untitled, 1977, Série Arbol de la vida (Tree of Life Series), colour photography documenting earth / body work with cloth, Oaxaca, Mexico, 133$^{1}/_{4}$" by 20" : 158-159h.

Jacket :
Front: Giraudon
Back: Dagli Orti

Colour separation
by PR Service Graphique

Printed in France
by MAME, Tours